EMPLOYMENT RELATIONS AND THE SOCIAL SCIENCES

STUDIES IN INDUSTRIAL RELATIONS

Hoyt N. Wheeler and Roy J. Adams, General Editors

EMPLOYMENT RELATIONS AND THE SOCIAL SCIENCES

Stephen M. Hills

UNIVERSITY OF SOUTH CAROLINA PRESS

Published in Columbia, South Carolina by the
University of South Carolina Press

Manufactured in the United States of America

Library of Congress Cataloging-in-Publication Data

Hills, Stephen M.
   Employment relations and the social sciences / Stephen M. Hills.
     p.   cm. — (Studies in industrial relations)
   Includes bibliographical references and index.
   ISBN 1–57003–035–9
   1. Industrial relations. 2. Industrial relations—Methodology.
I. Title. II. Series.
HD6961.H53 1995
331—dc20   95–4337

To Jack Barbash for his early inspiration
and
to Richard Bell for his friendship

CONTENTS

Figures   *viii*

Preface   *ix*

Introduction   *1*

Chapter 1: Social Sciences and the Employment Relationship   *7*

Chapter 2: Origins of the Field of Industrial Relations   *37*

Chapter 3: Marxism, Economics, and Industrial Relations   *50*

Chapter 4: Social Systems, Conflict, and Change   *61*

Chapter 5: Neo-institutionalists, Economics, and Industrial Relations   *90*

Chapter 6: The Psychologists and Industrial Relations   *114*

Chapter 7: Industrial Relations and the Social Sciences:
　　　　　The Long View   *131*

Notes   *147*

Bibliography   *149*

Index   *157*

FIGURES

Figure 1.1. Human Resource Activity   *15*

Figure 1.2. Development Activities   *21*

Figure 1.3. Allocation Activities   *26*

Figure 1.4. Utilization Activities   *29*

Figure 1.5. Maintenance Activities   *33*

PREFACE

The concept of this book came to me more than a decade ago. At that time, I joined several colleagues at the Ohio State University in a challenging, but very satisfying, series of discussions directed at how to integrate the field of industrial relations for graduate students who were just beginning their work. As a result of our discussions, a course was designed which purposefully straddled many of the usual dividing lines among the social sciences. With training in economics and industrial relations, I team-taught the course with a social psychologist. We alternated lectures throughout the quarter with each one critiquing the other's viewpoint at the end of each lecture. Students in the class were invited to join in these critiques. This classroom experience was one of the most satisfying I have had—filled with much intellectual challenge and enjoyment. After teaching the same survey course for a number of years, I saw the need for a framework that would help relate each of the social science disciplines to the fields of industrial relations and human resource management. This book is the result. I thank my colleagues for their inspiration and unwitting background collaboration in this project—Clif Kelley and Herbert Parnes with training in economics, Don Ronchi in social psychology, Rob Heneman in human resources, and Don Sanders in education. Goldie Shabad in political science and Bill Form in sociology were also helpful to me at various stages. I am grateful to a number of graduate students (in particular, Charles Smith) who read the book in earlier drafts and critiqued its message. Finally, my thanks to Roy Adams and Hoyt Wheeler for their long-standing support and encouragement in this task.

EMPLOYMENT RELATIONS
AND THE SOCIAL SCIENCES

INTRODUCTION

Since the early part of the twentieth century, the labor union has provided the field of industrial relations with a good part of its intellectual mooring, particularly in the United States. The industrial relations centers that were set up in American universities in the late 1930s and early 1940s focused their research and teaching on the dramatic growth of labor unions at the time. According to Jacoby, it was not surprising that early industrial relations centers focused attention on the labor movement since "the labor question, broadly defined, was arguably the most pressing problem in American society throughout the first half of this century, long after most other nations had adapted to trade unionism and the modern welfare state" (Jacoby 1988b; Jacoby 1993, 400). In this book, I will deal extensively with the labor question by relating it to a variety of social science traditions, but the labor union itself will not necessarily be the center of attention.

Prior to the 1930s, industrial relations was not strongly linked to the labor movement. The academic study of industrial relations was, in fact, very much associated with labor economics: "The field was a melange whose dominant element came from economics, although it also covered industrial sociology, personnel administration, labor law, labor history, and industrial psychology. But except for psychology, none of these had yet developed into specialties firmly rooted in disciplines outside of economics" (Jacoby 1988b; Jacoby 1993, 400).

One of the earliest U.S. industrial relations scholars, John R. Commons (1862–1945), was a labor economist, but he differentiated himself from other economists of his time by stressing the importance of economic institutions—the labor union being one of the most important. He also differentiated himself from European scholars by de-emphasizing social class as a factor in the growth of American labor unions. After Commons, a long line of American scholars would place minimal attention on class relationships when analyzing the dynamics of the industrial workplace. Instead, they examined the effects of the market and of large-scale, bureaucratic firms on the relationships that existed between labor and management.

In the United States, institutional economists like Commons stressed the need to test economic theory in everyday work activities. The result was an industrial relations tradition that was quite descriptive, focusing on the major institutions that affected industrial relationships. But even at its most descriptive, American industrial relations literature could still be linked to a number of the more abstract social science traditions.

In some cases, U.S. industrial relations scholars challenged conventional wisdom in the social sciences, seeking to show that the applied world of labor relations did not comply well with accepted theory. This was particularly true of economists like Commons who objected to many of the theoretical propositions of neoclassical economic theory. In other cases, industrial relations scholars combed through the body of theoretical propositions that made up each of the social sciences, formulated hypotheses about the employment relationship, and tested them in the real world of labor, management, and government interactions. In all cases, the labor union was viewed as a key institution in the web of industrial relationships that was examined.

In many industrialized countries today, membership rates are declining and account for a smaller percentage of the workforce. If this continues and unions play a less significant role in the social and economic system, one might ask whether the propositions of industrial relations scholars are well enough formulated to be tested in situations where the labor union fails to provide a theoretical anchor. Is the field of industrial relations based on an accepted body of theory that can be tested in union and nonunion settings alike? In part due to its strong attachment to the social sciences, industrial relations is not a field devoid of theory, despite regular complaints about inadequately developed or rudimentary theoretical constructs. As examples of industrial relations theory, Adams (1988a) points to theories of industrial relations systems, bargaining theory, conflict theory, dual labor market theory, theories of internal labor markets, theories of union-management participation, theories to predict individual worker preferences for unionization, theories to understand the determinants of job satisfaction, and theories to "explain the appearance of unions as well as union growth, structure, ideology, strategy, militancy and role in industrial society" (Adams 1988a, 6).

In a recent book, a number of industrial relations scholars have combined their thinking to produce an overview of industrial relations theory that is quite comprehensive (Adams and Meltz 1993). Yet, it is still difficult to create an integrated conceptual framework for analyzing the employment relationship, particularly one that might apply to both unionized and nonunionized settings. United States' industrial relations scholars are not readily identified with a consistent body of theory such as price theory in economics, motivation theory in psychology, or class theory in sociology. Furthermore, the use of the phrase—

U.S. industrial relations scholars—betrays the fact that industrial relations thought differs considerably from one country to another, and from one region of the world to another. Country-specific institutions have affected industrial relations thinking more than in the separate social sciences from which industrial relations thought has been drawn.

A general theoretical framework is needed to organize the wide variety of concepts and propositions that comprise the field of industrial relations, perhaps one that would complement or extend the systems' view of industrial relations proposed by Dunlop in 1958. This book tries to create such a framework, linking the social sciences with the industrial relations thought that has been derived from them. The framework has been designed to free the insights of industrial relations scholars from the peculiarities of country-specific institutions. It has as its reference point the employment relationship, not the labor union.

The analysis of employment relationships in the field of industrial relations need not be so strongly tied to labor unions or to the historical development of labor movements within specific countries. Karl Marx, undoubtedly one of the most influential social scientists to have lived, analyzed industrial work relationships without reference to unions. The same could be said for Max Weber. At the time that each wrote their theories (the early and mid-nineteenth century), labor unions did not play as significant a societal role as they would fifty to one hundred years later. Twentieth-century institutional economists, on the other hand, wrote during years of rapid union growth, but they still viewed the labor union as only one of several labor market institutions appropriate for testing their theories. A return to the writings of these scholars should help establish the core ideas on which industrial relations rests, whether or not the labor union is viewed as a key actor in the system.

A central proposition of this book is that industrial relations scholars have a unique outlook on the employment relationship, one that is not necessarily shared by the social sciences from which industrial relations theory is derived. A further presumption is that the field of industrial relations has boundaries that overlap many of the traditional social sciences. But what is meant by industrial relations? Some have defined the field in close association with the institutions it studies. For example, Flanders described industrial relations as the study of the institutions of job regulation (Hyman 1975, 11). By assuming that jobs need regulation, Flanders implicitly assumes that work itself had its tensions, its conflicts, and its contradictions. But the resolution, for Flanders, was a set of institutionalized rules and regulations which implied that the maintenance of stability and regularity was an underlying value premise of the study of industrial relations. This may or may not be true.

Margerison took a similar approach, but one that directly emphasized both the interactions of individuals and the institutional controls implied by a contract: "Industrial relations is the study of people . . . interacting in the doing of work in relation to some form of contract, either written or unwritten" (Margerison 1969, 274). The contract is an institutional arrangement, but the emphasis on the verb, interacting, means that Margerison's definitional focus has added the study of behavioral relationships in industry to the study of specific industrial institutions.

Richard Hyman (1975, 12) shifted the emphasis even further: "Industrial relations is the study of the processes of control over work relations, and among these processes, those involving collective worker organization and action are of particular concern."

Hyman's definition linked the employment relationship (not just the institutions of labor, management, and government) with control processes that could be examined from several social science perspectives. The definitions of Flanders, Margerison, and Hyman are similar, but they differ in the degree to which institutions, behavior, or control processes are emphasized. In this book, it will be argued that an understanding of control processes is a prerequisite for understanding the dynamics of industrial relationships. But the study of control should not be construed as exclusively Marxist—the control of the market, the control of protective institutions, the democratic control of unions and business enterprises, and the potential control of one class over another will be examined equally.

Throughout this book, reference is sometimes made to industrial relations scholars. Included within this group are early institutional economists like John R. Commons and Selig Perlman. These scholars would undoubtedly agree with Flanders that theirs is the study of the institutions of job regulation. Other more recent institutional economists (Dunlop, Kerr, Harbison, Myers, Somers) might also feel comfortable with Flanders' description of their area of interest, but might also find Margerison's definition too limiting. The work of these institutional economists often goes beyond work done under contract—even work done under an implicit contract. The analysis of social insurance, job training, job matching, and unemployment may be related to implicit political contracts, but have little to do with the kinds of contracts that come about through collective bargaining. Here I include present-day institutional economists as industrial relations scholars, as long as their work is directed at the institutions of job regulation.

Most of the above industrial relations scholars are (or were) economists. But to limit the term *industrial relations scholars* to economists seems inappropriate, especially since much analysis of employment relationships has occurred through other social science disciplines—psychology, sociology, and political science, for example. Here, Richard Hyman's definition of industrial relations is particularly useful. He argues that "collective worker organization and action" will always be a central concern to students of industrial relations, but that included among industrial relations scholars are those whose work is directed at "the process of control over work relations" (1975, 12). Presumably such scholars would not view collective worker action as illegitimate, given its central place in the field. But with that caveat, a student of human resource management or organizational behavior might well also be considered an industrial relations scholar. What links all such scholars together is their concern for the processes of control over work relations.

This book's central purpose is to demonstrate the connections between industrial relations and a whole variety of social science disciplines whose contributions to the field have not always been fully recognized. The plan for the book is to begin with a discussion of those scholars whose influence on the field has been well accepted. This approach leads one to examine the development of ideas historically, starting with Karl Marx and the institutional economists. But I move from there to other areas within the social sciences that have not been as closely associated with industrial relations. A number of sociologists are discussed, and then political scientists. Following this discussion, I turn to modern-day economists who define themselves as neo-institutionalists and end by discussing the contributions of psychologists who, though with considerable influence, have not necessarily been viewed as industrial relations scholars themselves. A conceptual framework is developed to integrate the ideas of this wide-ranging group of scholars.

The book's review of interconnections between social science theory and industrial relations serves several important purposes. First, it underscores those aspects of the employment relationship that will or will not lead to the growth and development of unions. Applied to the newly developing countries of Africa, Asia, and Latin America, social science theory then helps predict when and where labor movements are apt to occur. Secondly, the review helps in understanding the difficulties inherent in employment relationships, whether in preindustrial, industrial or so-called post-industrial societies—whether in societies where unions are strong or in societies where unions are weak or nonexistent. In serving these two purposes, however, the review also reveals sharp differences in outlook across the social sciences.

The differences in perspective are inherent in most industrial relations programs of study and are reflected in the coursework that students undertake. In some courses, the workforce is portrayed as divided among conflicting groups or classes, and the resolution of conflict is seen in the broader context of social change. In other courses, the workforce is depicted as a human resource to be screened, developed, motivated, and used by organizations. In the former case, conflict is typically viewed positively—as a catalyst for necessary adjustment and change. In the latter case, conflict may be viewed negatively—as an obstacle to the efficient use of human resources. These outlooks are based on well-developed social science theory, but their implications are not always complementary. This book addresses the contradictions of competing industrial relations outlooks with yet a third purpose in mind: to encourage students of industrial relations to cross disciplinary lines and to compare, integrate (if possible), and debate the principles of human behavior as set forth in each of the traditional disciplines.

Chapter 1

SOCIAL SCIENCES AND THE EMPLOYMENT RELATIONSHIP

Industrial society did not develop without its share of problems. Playwrights, novelists, and historians documented the traumatic changes in British society that occurred during the industrial revolution. The accounts in Charles Dickens' novels of life among the poor in nineteenth-century England, for example, are both vivid and compelling. But to give dimension to the employment relationship during the industrial revolution, one needs a more specific account of the experiences that all industrial workers must have shared, whether poor or not. Such an account is given by the historian, Karl Polanyi, who described in detail the agonizing transformation that occurred as feudal societies became industrialized. In a terse summary, he stated that "the effects on the lives of people were awful beyond description" (Polanyi 1957, 76). He went on to say:

> In disposing of a man's labor power the system [of uncontrolled markets in early industrial society] would, incidentally, dispose of the physical, psychological, and moral entity "man" attached to that tag. Robbed of the protective covering of cultural institutions, human beings would perish from the effects of social exposure; they would die as the victims of acute social dislocation through vice, perversion, crime, and starvation. . . . No society could stand the effects of such a system of crude fictions even for the shortest stretch of time unless its human and natural substance as well as its business organization was protected against the ravages of this satanic mill. (Polanyi 1957, 73)

For Polanyi, the ill effects of the industrial revolution were not so much the bad conditions under which the poor lived and worked (their poverty), but rather the dislocations suffered by workers who were no longer protected by cultural institutions. Polanyi attributed such dislocations (physical, psychological, and moral) to the unregulated operation of competitive markets. Polanyi's views differed sharply from the views of classical economists like Adam Smith whose book *Wealth of Nations* (1776) extolled the virtues of competitive markets as a means to rapid economic growth. Was the problem of a rapidly industrializing society a problem of unregulated markets as Polanyi contends? Or was it a problem of poverty? The argument continues today as countries of the former communist world reintroduce markets after industrialization has occurred. Will these markets be unregulated? Will protective institutions of the communist era (long-term guaranteed employment, universal health insurance) be retained in one form or another? Which new protective institutions (independent labor unions, unemployment insurance) should be developed?

Conflict in Employment Relationships:
Two Quite Different Solutions

Polanyi's views and those of classical economists are an appropriate starting point for examining industrial relations theory, once one accepts that industrialization and its system of competitive markets had (and still have) ill effects on employment relationships. In broad outline, this is the labor problem that industrial relations scholars have analyzed—a problem that is addressed by several of the social sciences. These social sciences provide the tools to measure the ill effects of industrialization, to uncover the causes of these effects, and to examine the dynamics that occur as individuals and groups have resisted the processes of industrialization.

A critical difference between industrial society and the feudal society that preceded it was the high degree of uncertainty accepted by individuals as they sold their labor services through a system of markets. This strong sense of individual insecurity stemmed from the establishment of a market economy. The most important ill effects of industrialization did not arise just from the machine technology of the industrial revolution, the one-company towns, the use of child labor, or the bad working conditions in early factories. These were superficial manifestations of the problem. Rather, the ill effects were a product of an oversupply of labor that was released from the agricultural sector to be used in newly developing industrial enterprises. Unskilled labor, in particular, faced tremendous uncertainty in the external labor market and an autocratic system of control in the workplace. The free market had produced a set of social relationships that could not permanently be tolerated (Polanyi 1957, 75). Nineteenth-century European history documents repeated attempts by individuals to protect their employment relationships from the influence of free markets (Polanyi 1957, 40). Individuals created the protective institutions that were ultimately to be taken for granted in the early part of the twentieth century: labor unions, unemployment and health insurance, social insurance of all kinds, labor market regulations, and centralized governmental planning. Here one must accept Polanyi's most important assertion—that individuals in a market economy will tolerate only a certain degree of social exposure before they seek protection from the market through institutional arrangements. Industrial relations theory comes into being when it is assumed that employment relationships in industrial (as well as post-industrial) society are problematic.

Today, economic systems are again faced with an over-supply of labor, but this time on a worldwide scale. This over-supply is comprised of people of widely differing cultures whose mobility is not just from agricultural sectors toward newly industrializing sectors of the economy. To be sure, in many countries the labor mobility of the first industrial revolution is being played out again, but in others, labor mobility is from less developed to more developed economies. Governments can constrain such mobility through immigration controls, but they cannot constrain the already industrialized firms from tremendous mobility in a world economy connected by rapid information flows and decreasing costs of transportation. In the more developed economies, the protective institutions that have been carefully constructed to deal with the ill effects of each country's industrialization are now under attack. Employment relationships again show strains that would be more than familiar to a historian like Polanyi.

Polanyi's perspective is evolutionary—problematic employment relationships can be reformed by regulation or modification of the market economy. An alternative perspective argues that the market system must be replaced in a revolutionary way. Marxist writers believe that employment relationships are problematic because an entire capitalist class has interests diametrically opposed to the interests of workers. To maintain their class position, capitalists will exploit the productive power of the workforce. In the meantime, capital will become ever more concentrated in the hands of the few, and unemployment will grow as a response to new technology. As in Polanyi's analysis, economic uncertainty results in a demand for change in the system, but the change will not be evolutionary. In Marxist analysis, the power of the few, the separation of interests along class lines, and the feelings of exploitation and alienation among the working class result in a demand for revolutionary change.

In Marxist analysis, the conflict within the firm and the conflict within the larger society are both highly interrelated. Marx examined in great detail the employment relationship between the owner of a firm and the worker. But he also examined the power relationships between employers as a class and workers in the broader society. He then made predictions for the playing out of conflict as workers united to seek change in the entire social and economic system. Polanyi's more evolutionary perspective also applied to the firm and to the broader society. For both Polanyi and Marx, employment relationships are problematic for individuals at work in their own industrial enterprises as well as for society as a whole.

In today's political world, Marxist ideas are in disrepute because of their association with discredited communist regimes. Planned economies that were called Marxist are rapidly being replaced by market economies that vary greatly in the degree of regulation these economies impose on business enterprises. It would be a serious mistake, however, to associate Marxist ideas solely with the discredited political systems of Communism. Marx's influence as a social scientist could well outlast even his extremely strong influence on world politics. For students of industrial relations, Marxist ideas form a significant part of the theory of employment relationships on which industrial relations theory is based.

Conceptualizing and Categorizing Employment Relationships

The discipline of economics has benefited from diagrammatic depiction of the theory underlying prices. The familiar supply and demand curves can be used to show changes in prices over time. They also illustrate the relationship between supply and demand as one exceeds the other (excess supply and excess demand). Adjustments in the market behavior of workers, consumers, and firms can be seen by understanding how supply and demand curves shift and relationships change. Finally, the relationships are sufficiently precise that they can be expressed mathematically as well as diagrammatically. Industrial relations theory could well benefit from a similar type of diagrammatic explanation of the variety of employment relationships that exist in industrial society.

A diagrammatic picture of the employment relationships would be quite useful if it could clarify the importance of both protection (Polanyi) and control (Marx) in market systems. But a depiction of the employment relationship should satisfy at least five other criteria as well.

The first criterion is that the conceptualization should be readily applicable to the everyday activities of the workplace. It is tempting to formulate a picture for industrial relations as derived from "grand theory." In John Dunlop's classic formulation, the industrial relations system was depicted through the interactions of three main actors—labor, management, and government—who were bound together by a web of rules that governed the system. In this formulation, the system is more or less viewed from the top down and is akin to the tripartite view of the economic system derived from macro-economics.

In macro-economic theory, total economic activity is equal to the sum of consumption, investment, and government expenditure, or $Y = C + I + G$. Yet macro-theory is insufficient for predicting the course of the system through time without a keen understanding of the dynamics of a myriad of individual relationships—the pricing activity of workers, consumers, and firms, derived from economics; the work group or local community behaviors of individuals, from sociology; the voting behaviors of individuals, from political science; and, from psychology, individual attitudes and motivations. In industrial relations, a total industrial relations system can certainly be envisioned for a given country and perhaps for the world as well. But it is difficult to understand the grand strategies of the actors in the system without first starting with the key elements of an individual's employment relationship and then expanding one's focus to the work unit, the firm, government, and society as a whole.[1]

The second criterion is that the conceptualization should clearly show the impact of government policy on the workplace. Application of industrial relations theory has typically occurred in countries with mixed economies where market forces are important but where government policy regulates the market significantly (an outcome Polanyi predicts). The conceptualization should provide some indication as to why industrial relations theory is helpful under circumstances of government regulation and control over the market. It should also clarify the way in which government policy affects individual employment relationships.

The third criterion is that the conceptualization should provide some common ground for debate between Marxist and non-Marxist theorists. Politically, a tremendous change toward pragmatism rather than ideology has occurred in countries previously committed to Marxist politics. A corresponding pragmatism regarding conceptualization in industrial relations theory would be highly desirable—incorporating ideas in common to both Marxist and non-Marxist scholars. A concept that is used by both groups is control. A conceptualization that emphasized control processes but allowed for different interpretations of control would therefore be quite desirable.

The fourth criterion is that the conceptualization should illustrate, at least to some degree, the dynamics of negotiation. Negotiation is a key process in virtually all the employment relationships analyzed by industrial relations theory. And it is being increasingly incorporated into theory that derives from several of the social sciences: economics, political science, psychology, and sociology. Consequently, a better understanding of the negotiation process for individuals and groups should enhance one's understanding of the dynamics of the entire industrial relations system.

The final criterion is that the conceptualization should be readily linked to the social sciences. If the conceptualization includes an emphasis on negotiation, a strong link to the social sciences is to some degree established due to the ongoing interest in the topic across the disciplines. If the conceptualization is specific enough in terms of workplace activities, it can also provide a strong connection to the social sciences by linking particular types of activity to each social science that treats this activity as an application of its theory. A particular social science discipline often emphasizes one set of workplace activities more than another. A good conceptualization can make these special emphases explicit.

An overall conceptual scheme for industrial relations should build industrial relations theory from the bottom up, starting with the key elements of an individual's employment relationship and then expanding its focus to the work unit, the firm, government, and society as a whole. But to simplify, it would be desirable to categorize the day-to-day activities that occur in the workplace. A simple, though inclusive, classification results in four main categories: (1) activities surrounding the education, training, and development of human resources; (2) activities related to the allocation of individuals to specific jobs; (3) activities that affect how individual energies are utilized once people have been matched with jobs; and (4) activities that influence the way in which work effort is maintained over time—in other words, the development, the allocation, the utilization, and the maintenance of human resources.

Each of the four human resource activities can occur within the confines of the business firm, within a local labor market, or within the larger economic community. Firms may be involved in cross training of their employees (development), job evaluation and human resource planning (allocation), performance appraisal (utilization), and employee assistance plans (maintenance). In the local labor market, schools train prospective employees in basic skills, the state employment service allocates job seekers to job openings, a local labor-management committee encourages employers and unions to cooperate with each other (thereby decreasing the number of strikes and increasing the effectiveness of business organizations), and a statewide system of worker's compensation protects employees and employers from the costs of injuries. At the national level, most governments help to fund national systems of apprenticeship or other post-secondary training. In the United States, the federal government pays for the cost of administering the employment service and the various statewide systems of unemployment compensation. In today's world, government often provides research funding directed at how to increase its own national productivity, and it is usually the national government's responsibility to provide insurance for older citizens (social security).

Institutions sponsor all of the above activities. These institutions do not come into existence automatically—they usually are built up through a long and arduous process by individuals who are convinced that the resulting activities will serve their own (or their children's) individual interests. The institutions operate in a complicated environment of conflicting interests that must be resolved—at times, through difficult negotiation. The institutional activities and negotiations that occur at every level within the economic system are the subject matter of the field of industrial relations.

The four main activities that comprise the employment relationship have now been defined, but to stop here would leave the conceptualization descriptive and static. The dynamics of industrial relations revolve around the problem of who or what controls the employment relationship, and it is around this issue that some of the most difficult negotiations occur. On the one hand, there are those who argue that the employment relationship can and should be controlled impersonally through a competitive, free market. Classical economists like Adam Smith and neoclassical economists like Milton Friedman would definitely make such an argument. In the unregulated, free-market system that they envision, individuals make decisions about the development, allocation, utilization, and maintenance of their human resources, but very little control is assumed for institutions like government, labor unions, or labor-management committees. Government is assumed to play a small role in the economy, and business firms are envisioned to be small in size and competing vigorously with each other. Some firms succeed because of the choices they make in response to market signals, and others fail because they ignore the information they receive from the market. Unions are, according to this view, an obstacle to the efficient operation of the market and should be avoided if possible.

At another extreme, quite a different view prevails if a system of monopoly capitalism operates instead of the free-market system. In this case, the locus of control does not solely reside in the market. Large, powerful firms, instead, subsume a great deal of the control over the system. In the competitive, free-market system, the firm served as an agent for fulfilling the desires of consumers and employees alike. The firm created the products from which consumers could choose. The firm also created the jobs from which individuals could choose. If an individual were to try out a job and find it unsatisfactory, a switch could readily be made to another firm that would, in turn, serve as an agent for the individual's satisfaction in work, income, and wealth. But if the firm grows large and powerful and becomes immune to market constraints (becomes a monopoly), it may no longer serve as an agent for the desires of the individuals who work in it, or, for that matter, for the desires of the consumers who buy from it. Instead, the firm may serve primarily the interests of those who own and/or control it. The firm will create for itself an independent locus of control so that the market is not exclusively in control of the employment relationship. Thus, there are two polar opposite possibilities for control—one centered exclusively in the market and championed by classical economists, the other centered exclusively in monopoly firms and challenged by the Marxist. Industrial relations, as a field, assumes that there are many other intermediate possibilities for control, with a variety of labor market institutions assuring that neither of the extreme situations will prevail. Industrial relations scholars argue that when one looks at what is really happening in economies of the world, neither extreme for control of the employment relationship exists. Instead, a quite complex set of institutional arrangements governs how people become employed, how they relate to their employers, and how they live once retired.

The structure of control in industrial societies shapes the negotiation that individuals can undertake with regard to their own employment relationships. In a competitive, free-market system, very little negotiation is possible since small firms simply create specific jobs that are required to create a product or provide a service. Individuals look over the jobs available and more or less take them or leave them. Likewise, in a world of monopoly capitalism, individuals have little room for negotiation. An individual's power to negotiate is relatively small compared to the power of the firm. But negotiation is possible if individuals, through agents that they create (labor unions or works councils, for example), resist the concentration of control either in the market or in the hands of a monopoly firm's owners or management.

It is argued here that if the locus of control over the employment relationship is centered totally in the market or in the firm, individuals will seek out or create agents to protect themselves from the negative consequences of such control. Control that is concentrated in the market is undesirable because technological change or changes in consumer preferences often require rapid changes in the four human resource activities. New products may require quite different skills for employees. Some products may no longer be demanded so firms will die and employees will have to find new jobs. An unregulated, free-market system demands that such changes be made quickly, a process that is often painful for individuals. Yet control that is concentrated wholly in the firm is also undesirable because it restricts the choices that individuals can make and requires change according to the dictates of the employer.

Agents that can help to ease the pain of adjustment to change in the employment relationship are exemplified by the following: a labor union that establishes contractual regulations for a variety of management-initiated decisions about work, a council of elected employees that participates with management in establishing workplace policies, a government that supports the establishment of labor unions or requires works councils in business firms, a government-operated firm that can slow the pace of change, or a joint labor-management committee that writes procedural rules for administering unemployment compensation, worker's compensation, or government-sponsored training programs. In each of these cases negotiation will be required, but the agent is assumed to be transparent in the process of negotiation by reflecting the interests of individual constituents. The agent represents a group of individuals, thereby increasing any one individual's ability to control the employment relationship—control that would otherwise accrue to the firm or to the market.

Unfortunately, agents who are transparent and always represent the individual interests of constituents may belong to the academic's ideal world. In reality, the protective agents that employees create may, at times, represent themselves—labor union leaders, government civil servants, and others. A new potential locus of control over the employment relationship has been created, one from which individuals may, in turn, also need protection. One way to achieve such protection is to return to market forces as the basic means of control, eliminating a union-controlled hiring hall for example, and allowing employers to select their workforce from the labor market without requiring that union members alone be hired. Another means of protection is for one agent to control another—for government to exercise control over labor unions by requiring the use of democratic procedures in the election of officers, for example. Public employees themselves may unionize to protect themselves from the power of government.

To summarize the argument so far, industrial relations is the study of the negotiation of individuals or their agents about control over the employment relationship. The negotiation deals with the specific problems of developing, allocating, using, and maintaining human resources. Firms, labor organizations, and government may all be used by individuals to protect themselves from the market. But each of these agents may also become a center of control. Constant negotiation prevents any one center of control from predominating over the full set of employment relationships. With this argument in hand, it is possible to sketch out a summary picture of the full set of employment relationships that exist in an economic system. The picture needs to be multidimensional both to incorporate the important concept of control and to allow for the continuous negotiation of a variety of labor market institutions.

Figure 1.1

Human Resource Activity: Development, Allocation, Utilization, or Maintenance
By Center of Control

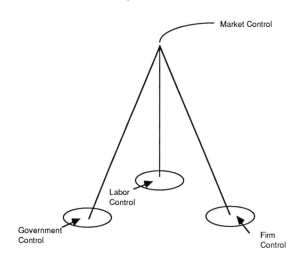

Figure 1.1 has been drawn to show the interaction among various centers of control over the employment relationship and the four functional areas that comprise employment related activities. For each functional area, lines radiate out from a market-centered locus of control to three other potential control centers. Within each control center, at least one key labor market institution operates.

The market itself is quite an important institution—it is the set of rules and regulations governing pricing behavior that in turn allows potential buyers and sellers to communicate effectively with one another even though they may be separated by physical distances and communicate only in writing, by phone, or by computer. The key institution in the control center labeled labor is the labor union, but others might be works councils or professional associations. Within the United States, the control center labeled government includes the private industry councils that set local training policies; the advisory committees that help to set policy for worker's compensation, unemployment insurance, and a host of other government activities directed toward the labor market; and the civil service bureaucracies of such agencies as the U.S. Department of Labor or the Social Security Administration.

The negotiation that individuals engage in through any one of these institutions determines whether control will be concentrated in only one center or whether control will be shared among two or more centers of control. The "higgling and haggling" over price described by Adam Smith is but one form of negotiation in the world of industrial relations. Negotiations over the terms of a labor contract, over grievances, over the regulations of worker's compensation, or over determining the proper mix of training services offered by government are all legitimately studied within the field. Notice that with the exception of price determination in the market, the negotiations are all done through institutions that serve as agents for the individuals who have created them.

If government or labor served only as agents for individuals, they would be transparent in figure 1.1. No lines would be drawn to show separate centers of control for either of them. Instead, government or labor agents would simply assist individuals in negotiating a system of control that was neither totally centered in the firm nor in the market. The results of negotiation would be shown somewhere in the middle of the axis that connects the firm to the market, a position of shared control between workers and their employers. As drawn, however, figure 1.1 shows that both government and labor may also vie for control over the employment relationship and potentially could acquire complete control. If either gained total control, what would be the consequence?

A centralization of control over the employment relationship in government has, in the past, usually been associated with authoritarianism—a situation that precludes negotiation altogether. Communist central planning exemplifies this type of control, but it is also an arrangement that has been strongly resisted—as witnessed by the dramatic events that have occurred in Eastern Europe and in the former Soviet Union. Experience with communist central planning shows that if government is to retain an agency function and to further the interests of individual employees, it must at least to some degree be democratic to check potential abuse of its far-reaching authority.

Whether democratic or not, a high degree of government control over the employment relationship may unduly restrict the firm's ability to respond to the market. Employers may be required to hire those sent them by government agencies and to maintain them in employment for life. Individuals may lose the choice over jobs that market-directed control over the employment relationship would provide, and employers may sacrifice production efficiency, thereby reducing growth in the economic system.

Control over the employment relationship that is concentrated wholly in union leaders' hands would have many of the same results described for government control through central planning. Unions would own and direct economic enterprises and would be subject to the same potential abuses that can occur under central planning. Unions should therefore also be democratic to avoid abuse of their authority and to retain their agency functions. Though total control over the employment relationship by labor is theoretically possible, real-life examples are hard to find. One does, however, find situations where government and labor join forces to exercise joint control over the employment relationship—Juan Peron's corporatist government in Argentina, for example (Schmitter and Lehmbruch 1979).

When control rests exclusively in the market, negotiation over a comprehensive employment relationship is not as important as the process of defining individual jobs and contracting for them to be filled. To understand how an employment relationship is established, the free-market economist does not examine how individuals or groups negotiate conflict, but rather looks to how markets help resolve conflict. For the free-market economist, the worker joins a firm (a group) only after marketing individually developed skills; the skills are fitted into the production process once the individual accepts a job that best uses those skills. Individuals work out potential conflicts for themselves by making careful choices in the market, and ultimately choose jobs that are a compromise between the needs of the employer (as set out in a detailed job description) and their own needs. Workers must know in advance what the choices are, make rational decisions, contract with employers to fill the requirements of specific jobs, and then accommodate to them. If economic circumstances change, the employer may change job requirements. Employees must then recontract to fill the new positions or quit and search the market for new jobs, where once again they will be contracted to adjust to the needs of the employer. When control is vested totally in the market, employers search intermittently for prospective employees who are willing to accept predetermined jobs and then to accommodate to them. The only negotiation that occurs is over the wage rate.

As in the case where control is concentrated in government, individuals may strongly resist the concentration of control in the market. When markets operate without regulation, individuals are often unable and unwilling to accept the constant accommodation required of them and will negotiate institutional protection. These individuals will seek out long-term employment contracts with individual firms—either detailed written agreements or simple implicit understandings. Additionally, these individuals will organize unions and lobby government for protective legislation and social insurance. The institutional protections thus created will surround each impersonal job description with a set of very personal expectations and understandings, established by groups in the defense of their individual interests. Management and unions reach understandings about the proper pace of work, about appropriate ways to carry out work, and about the conditions under which work will be done. Government legislation creates norms for health and safety and for treatment of minorities. When offering long-term employment contracts, firms may ask employees to be flexible about future job assignments in exchange for job security. All such negotiated understandings and agreements create an ever-changing employment relationship that takes the place of the fixed, contractually determined jobs envisioned by free-market theory. The ever-changing and negotiated employment relationship is derived from a world of shared control between government and the market, between the labor union and the market, and between the firm and the market. In this world of shared control, the conditions of employment are negotiated in addition to the wage.

Marxist scholars describe the outcome of yet a third extreme where control is held almost exclusively by capitalist firms. Marxist scholars argue that the market system does not adequately resolve conflict because imbedded in the system is the influence of social class. Since members of the upper class have disproportionate power in the market, they can restrict the choices of others. In other words, the upper class has control over the market. The job choices of individuals no longer represent a compromise between the interests of consumers and the preferences of job seekers. Instead, the best jobs are reserved for the upper classes. Upper-class members also have disproportionate control within the firm. Lower-class members of society must either accept work roles with limited autonomy and control or join the ranks of the unemployed. Class conflict results and with it comes a profound crisis for the entire economic system. Political behavior is the result, but with an aim to overturn the economic and social system.

Values and the Employment Relationship

The normative issues of industrial relations arise in relationship to policy: should capitalist firms be dismantled in an attempt to eliminate class control? Do individuals need protection from market control, from firm-level control, from the control of labor unions, and from government control? Or should individuals be primarily responsible for managing their own human resources? Under what circumstances should firms be restricted in the management of the human resources they control? Should a labor union control all the human resource decisions of the firm? The answers to such questions are reached societally, but due to strong beliefs about control, industrial relations scholars will often not remain totally neutral.

Industrial relations scholars argue that none of the extremes of control need occur, but the alternatives they suggest may reflect either a reformist or a radical view of the world. Reformists argue that total market control should yield to a system where control is shared with groups of individuals who, in turn, create institutions that help to shape the work environment (Commons 1961; Perlman 1949; Webb and Webb 1897). Individuals may, however, become controlled by the very institutions they create (Jacoby 1985). Government planning agencies, social insurance bureaucracies, large firms that provide long-term employment security, labor unions, and government regulatory agencies may themselves begin to assume a significant degree of control over the lives of individual employees. This control, likewise, will be resisted if too great, thus limiting the authority of public officials, labor union leaders, or private management (Storey 1983). Industrial relations scholars argue that the control of the market should not be totally replaced by government (or any other agent's) control over all areas of economic activity. Shared control is, instead, the objective.

Radicals argue that the control of powerful firms is more a threat to individuals than the control of the market system per se. And the control of monopoly firms will be resisted, not so much by building protective institutions as by revolutionary action (Gorz 1967; Burawoy 1978). Monopoly capitalism will be replaced by a system of central planning, but that control system should only be temporary. Eventually, the system would itself be transformed, leading to yet a better system.

The Importance of the Workplace

A discussion of reformist and radical policy alternatives has already established a connection between industrial relations and the social sciences, but to make the link more formal, the specific activities comprising each of the four areas (development, allocation, utilization, and maintenance of human resources) should be made more explicit. This explicitness is needed because research in the social sciences is directed at specific individual behaviors that must in turn be related to equally specific workplace activities. An enumeration of such activities should, nevertheless, retain the overall idea that these activities occur in the context of alternative centers of control.

Industrial relations scholars argue that too much control in the hands of management is highly undesirable. The most vocal of these, as already seen, are the Marxists with their emphasis on class divisions and conflict. Industrial relations scholars also oppose a concentration of control with labor or government. Some advocate union democracy as a necessary check on the power of union leaders (Sayles and Strauss 1967) and industrial democracy as an alternative to centralized planning (Carnoy and Shearer 1980). Industrial relations scholars also argue that too heavy a reliance on market control is to be avoided— the institutionalist school of thought representative of this type of market critique. By taking such positions, industrial relations scholars make explicit a set of values regarding the employment relationship, namely that too heavy an emphasis on any one center of control should be resisted.

In figures 1.2–1.5, examples of specific activities are enumerated for each category of workplace activity, but in such a way that potential centers of control can be recognized.[2] For activities that are nearest to each center of control, the possibility for negotiation is minimized; for those in the middle, negotiation over a wide range of issues is likely. Since industrial relations scholars believe that too heavy a concentration of control in any one center should be resisted, these scholars will be interested in workplace activities that have a high potential for negotiation and will place a higher value on the social science research that is directed at the activities listed in the middle range of each axis of control.

Human Resource Development:
Workplace Activities and Related Social Science Theory

The activities listed in figure 1.2 focus on processes for acquiring job-related skills, but the ways in which skills are acquired involve decisions by individuals, by their agents (government or unions) and by firms. In a market-driven economy, as seen above, firms may simply advertise for the skills they need, post a price, and wait for skilled individuals to respond. For the individual in a market-controlled situation, career development consists of a set of choices over time, made in response to market signals. This set of activities is illustrated as number five in figure 1.2—unregulated and unsubsidized individual choice of training.

The value system in industrial relations does not support control concentrated in the market alone. An unregulated and unsubsidized market that is changing

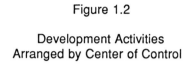

Figure 1.2

Development Activities
Arranged by Center of Control

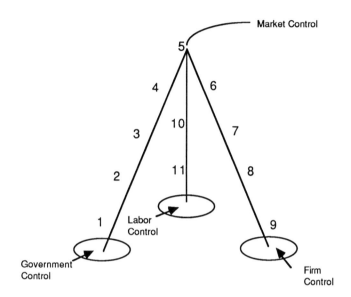

Human Resource Development Activities Shown in Figure 1.2 (Definition of Symbols)

1. Centralized government economic development planning with government-financed training institutions supplying a fixed number of trained persons per year to be placed in government-sponsored projects.
2. Government-financed compulsory education with individual choice of field based on individual preferences and potential future earnings.
3. Government-guaranteed loans to individuals who choose specific training programs within broad areas deemed to be acceptable (for example, guaranteed loans for college or university training).
4. Government-financed assistance in providing information about present and future job openings (so that individuals know what training to obtain privately).
5. Unregulated and unsubsidized individual choice of training programs as offered by private firms (individual career development).
6. Firm-sponsored training programs offered to employees. Programs that combine firm-specific training with general training that is transferable through the market.

Figure 1.2 (Definition of Symbols), **continued**

   7. Firm-sponsored, firm-specific training.
   8. Firm-directed promotions, work experience, and career development.
   9. Indentured servants.
   10. Joint apprenticeship programs—firm, union, and government.
   11. Union-sponsored apprenticeship with requirement to hire union approved
       apprentices alone

---

rapidly can create an intolerable degree of uncertainty for individuals, particularly when information about new job opportunities and careers is incomplete. Government-subsidized compulsory education is the first departure from a completely market-controlled career development system; this compulsory education guarantees that the workforce will have at least a minimum level of general skills to be used in making adjustments to market changes.[3] Government may also subsidize the costs of gaining job information by way of a public employment service, specialized training, and economic development planning. The progression to full government control is illustrated by specific activities four, three, two, and one in figure 1.2.

Enumeration of human resource development activities (as in figure 1.2) clarifies not only the type of social science theory that is critical for industrial relations scholars, but also some of the reasons for its importance. The economist's human capital theory is clearly important for any type of career development based on market choice, but it does not necessarily help one to understand why objections might arise to a system of elementary education paid for exclusively by educational vouchers. A voucher-based system brings into play a variety of interests: educators who feel comfortable with a system of control over curriculum that is based on their professional judgment and not necessarily the wishes of parents/consumers, government representatives who serve as agents for minorities to guarantee that a voucher system does not exclude their clients, and parents who may be dissatisfied with educational diversity or quality. The resulting negotiated solution to these conflicts of interest is a topic that is as amenable to the tools of analysis of the industrial relations scholar as it is amenable to the negotiated solution to a complicated labor contract. It is not a topic that should be analyzed exclusively through the lens of human capital theory.

A well-developed theory exists that applies to the extremes of human resource development activity depicted in figure 1.2—human capital theory. This theory applies equally well when control is centered in the market or when it is completely centered in government or the firm. A government planner or a firm's human resource planner can calculate the costs and benefits of additional investment (as can individuals), and human capital theory can guide each person's decisions. But the social science theory required for the middle range of human resource activities shown in figure 1.2 (activities two, three, and four) is less well developed. A well-developed theory that applied to the middle range of activities would rely both on conflict theory and theories of negotiation. Conflict theory specifies that conflict originates under conditions of cooperation or shared activity, but the parties involved have mutually exclusive objectives that cannot be achieved simultaneously (Schmidt and Kochan 1971). In the case of human resource development, the shared activities, the mutually exclusive objectives, and the institutions that would be expected to negotiate a settlement have not been spelled out in a well-developed theoretical framework. Theory has not been developed, for example, to analyze tripartite negotiations over the training provided to individuals at the local level of the U.S. economic system (the private industry councils) or of the Swedish system (the Labor Market Board).[4] Perhaps a better developed theory of conflict and negotiation would have facilitated implementation of President Johnson's War on Poverty program. The initial assumption seems to be that subsidized training services, if offered by government, will lift individuals from poverty. Too little attention has been paid to the need for agents to represent the poor in negotiating different economic rules of the game. Human capital theory is assumed to be sufficient to understand the choices that the poor will subsequently make among various types of subsidized and unsubsidized training services. Industrial relations theory, according to my conceptual framework, should cast doubt on this assumption and lead one to ask how individuals can improve their chances for training through negotiation.

Human resource development takes on a very different connotation if individuals are employed by large firms and if one examines the sharing of control among firms, labor unions (if they exist), and the market. The degree to which individual preferences are reflected in career development is often a matter for negotiation and is reflected in the progression of human resource activities depicted in figure 1.2 moving from total market to total firm control. In the case of a firm with a highly developed internal labor market, a human resource planning department may determine successors for specific jobs, controlling the promotion process throughout the firm. Training is provided for specific individuals in anticipation of promotion. Individuals, on the other hand, will usually prefer open competition for jobs based on a system of bidding that has clear criteria to determine the minimum requirements for a job vacancy. By knowing in advance which jobs are most likely to become vacant, individuals can train for them, thereby anticipating promotions to the jobs to which they aspire. The final shape of the firmwide training system is, thus, a matter for negotiation. If firms give general training, they will provide individuals with the means to resist managerial control since their skills can then be sold in the open market. Thus, firms would be expected to prefer training programs that apply more specifically to the firm, while individuals would prefer more general training. The conflict in interests sets the stage for negotiation.

A conflict of interests may also characterize union apprenticeship programs. Many apprenticeship programs are jointly directed by labor unions and employers, but in some cases (such as construction), union control over apprenticeship has led to conflict between the interests of individual union members and public policy. The requirement to hire only union-trained apprentices allows a craft union to restrict the supply of skilled workers, raise wages, and, in some cases, discriminate by race and gender. But if some individuals are excluded from training, government may attempt to control or bypass the apprenticeship system and increase directly the numbers of women and minorities represented by the crafts. Human capital theory is not as useful in understanding the interests of unions in apprenticeship as is an industrial relations theory that emphasizes power relationships and organizational structure and control.

The theory underlying firm-level negotiation of development activities is more developed than that for government-level negotiations. Three types of firm-level theories are significant. Human capital theory differentiates between general training and firm-specific training, as already seen above. This distinction allows one to identify managerial interests and control in providing specific training. The theory of internal labor markets differentiates between ports of entry where the external labor market exercises control and internal job ladders where individual and collective negotiation are critically important (Doeringer and Piore 1971). Finally, theories of human resource planning apply statistical models to the flows of people through various job positions in the organization and focus on the training required to facilitate such flows (Burack and Walker 1972). Less emphasized, however, has been the theoretical treatment of the power structure within the firm and its effect on negotiations over the human resource development activities of the firm or the labor union. Though better developed than theory dealing with government subsidized education and training, theories of conflict, negotiation, and control over firm-level human resource development activities could still benefit from additional elaboration.

Human Resource Allocation and Utilization:
Workplace Activities and Related Social Science Theory

Even a brief look at the activities included in figures 1.3 and 1.4 (allocation and utilization) shows that these are the areas of greatest theorizing and research in the field of industrial relations. Not surprisingly, the labor union serves an important representational function for institutions in both of these areas. It plays a prominent role in negotiation—both in establishing national public policy and at the local level where bargaining occurs over compensation, the terms of employment, working conditions, grievance procedures, and the introduction of new technology. To analyze human resource allocation and utilization activities, industrial relations scholars have developed an ample body of theory about unions—theories of union structure and governance, bargaining, and union-joining behavior, for example (Dunlop 1944; Kochan 1980; Sayles and Strauss 1967; Strauss 1977; Zeuthen 1930; Chamberlain 1951; Stevens 1963; Walton and McKersie 1965; Wheeler 1985). Underlying these theories are theories of conflict, thereby linking industrial relations directly to the social sciences where this topic is examined—sociology, in particular, but also political science and psychology. When unions are not a strong factor in negotiation, industrial relations scholars have developed theories that apply to managerial activity in the areas of compensation, performance appraisal, employee motivation, and job satisfaction. All of these theories underlie the conceptual framework presented in figures 1.3 and 1.4.

Figure 1.3 spells out a number of human resource activities that one would associate with the allocational functions of the market, the firm, and the government. At the top of the figure, where control is centered in the market, the job-matching activities that one associates with free, competitive labor markets are found. Here, standard economic theory explains both wage rate determination and the mobility of individuals across jobs. But listed between the market and each of the other centers of control are activities that depart to one degree or another from the rules of competitive labor markets. The activities listed moving from market to government control, for example, range from government-financed occupational projections to government-mandated hiring quotas. The theory underlying activity number five (occupational projections and other subsidized labor market information) is still derived from neoclassical theory. In this case, the role of government is to correct market imperfections by providing information. After the market imperfection has been removed, standard economic theory applies. When moving farther toward full government control over the employment relationship, standard economic theory is less applicable. Policies of affirmative action and comparable worth, for example, rest on the assumption that social relationships are more important to wage rate determination than is the market. The concept of a fair wage and the assumption that negotiated wage rates are required to remedy discrimination are key elements in a theory of comparable worth. Farther down the control axis one finds hiring quotas that could be viewed as part of government's function to protect the interests of specific subgroups of citizens. But if government is perceived as representing one group of citizens and not another, then quotas could be viewed as a means by which specific subgroups achieve their own coercive control over

Figure 1.3

Allocation Activities
Arranged by Center of Control

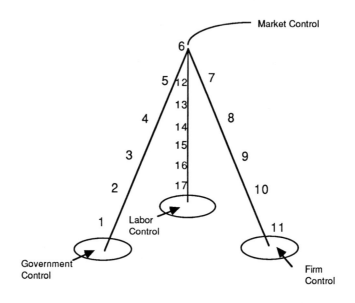

Human Resource Allocation Activities Shown in Figure 1.3
(Explanation of Symbols)

1. Government-controlled placement on all jobs. Government-designed compensation schedule.
2. Government-imposed hiring quotas and rules for determining compensation for race and gender groups in the private and public sectors.
3. Government-designed policies for pay based on the comparable worth of all public sector jobs.
4. Government-regulated affirmative action policies for selection, promotion, and pay within the public and private sectors.
5. Government-subsidized occupational projections, wage and salary information, and job-placement services.
6. Unregulated market-guided choice of jobs and establishment of compensation through forces of supply and demand. Individuals search freely for jobs. Firms search for prospective job applicants.
7. Internal job posting system where internal applicants compete freely with external applicants. Formalized job evaluation and performance appraisal for promotion and pay. Compensation based on a schedule that may be the result of a union contract.

Figure 1.3 (Explanation of Symbols), **continued**

    8. Internal job posting system where internal applicants are given first consideration for all but low-level positions. Formalized job evaluation and performance appraisal for promotion and pay. Compensation based on a schedule that may be the result of a union contract.

    9. Firm-level screening and job placement based on criteria that are not necessarily job related.

  10. Upper-level positions filled only from within with no formalized criteria for promotion and pay and no job posting.

  11. Slavery.

  12. Union-acquired information on job openings through contractually demanded job postings or through informal networks.

  13. Union-demanded system of promotions from within.

  14. Agency shop.

  15. Union shop.

  16. Closed shop.

  17. Hiring hall.

---

employment relationships. Quotas, in that case, could be appropriately depicted in a position closer to full government control.

    Economic job search theory undergirds a free-market view of job matching. In this extension of human capital theory (Lippman and McCall 1976), individuals who search for jobs consider both the costs and benefits of engaging in one additional search period. But other more sociological formulations of job search theory may also introduce two now-familiar ideas: control over information and negotiation to improve one's control. Information about new job possibilities can derive from informal networks that differ by race and gender, for example. Likewise, job information may accrue to an individual due to the characteristics of her/his current job. Some jobs are rich in information about other work opportunities while other jobs are not (Granovetter 1974). Negotiation may be helpful to achieve a more favorable position in the information network. Labor unions, women's support groups, or support groups for the unemployed are examples of the institutions that could play an important role in negotiating better access to information (activity twelve of figure 1.3).

    In figure 1.3, allocational activities eight, nine, and ten are shown midway between total market and total firm control over job allocation. These activities are closely associated with the idea of an internal labor market—a market created within the firm by rules restricting the hiring of new employees from outside. If firms are small and competitive, they do not typically develop internal labor markets, and they have little independent control over individuals. In modern capitalist economies, however, large bureaucratic firms with highly developed internal labor markets have devised a system which provides a significant degree of protection for individuals through long-term employment contracts. Individuals have often sought additional protection through their own agents—labor unions. Unions demand written rules for promotion, for layoffs, and for hiring or rehiring. These unions help to create an internal labor market in which managerial flexibility over allocation and utilization of labor is controlled. Management prefers flexibility and autonomy in judging performance while employees prefer clear and measurable criteria for evaluation. Classic conflict thus develops setting the stage for a negotiated settlement.

In figure 1.3, unions are shown to represent individuals in several different ways as they demand better methods for allocating jobs. At the firm level, for example, unions may demand that job openings be made available to everyone through public posting of positions or they may demand that all promotions be made from within (activities number twelve and thirteen in figure 1.3). But activities closer to the position of centralized labor control show how representational activities can be replaced by activities that reinforce the union organization itself. Closed shop provisions and hiring halls may serve individual interests by providing secure employment for union members, but they may also serve to enhance the power of the union's leadership and open up the possibility for abuse of the union's power.

Note that in figure 1.3, as in all the figures, the term *labor union,* can mean either a public or private sector union. In the field of industrial relations, a significant amount of theory has been developed to apply specifically to public sector negotiation. For figures 1.3 and 1.4 in particular, the theory applies to activities that occur when government is in control of the employment relationship, directly negotiating compensation and allocating individuals across its own public sector jobs. To some degree, theories developed for private sector bargaining can simply be transferred to the public sector. But because of the nonprofit nature of public sector employment, theories of tripartite bargaining (Kochan 1974; Derber 1988)—or theories of dispute resolution that focus on alternatives to the strike—have also been developed. In many of these theories, the important question is who ultimately has managerial control over a negotiated contract—whether the vaguely defined concept of government is sufficient or whether the electorate broadly defined should be considered to be in control. In either case, industrial relations scholars would argue that negotiated settlement of the terms of employment is better than total government control since government may not serve solely as an agent for the electorate and become, instead, a center of control itself.

The utilization activities shown in figure 1.4 are concerned with the best fit of individuals to jobs at any one point in time. They differ from the allocational activities considered in figure 1.3 because there the movement from one job to another occurs over time. For the firm, good utilization of human resources at

Figure 1.4

Utilization Activities
Arranged by Center of Control

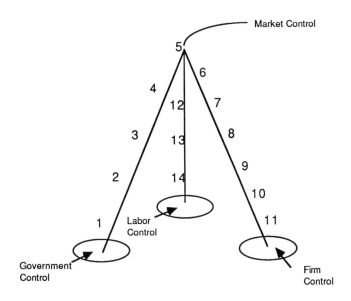

Human Resource Utilization Activities Shown in Figure 1.4
(Explanation of Symbols)

1. Centralized government control over investment decisions, technological change, and the way in which labor is combined with capital.
2. Governmental guidance over industrial restructuring. Subsidies to selected firms which, without assistance, would go bankrupt.
3. Government research on the effects of technological change and the best ways of easing labor force adjustment problems to that change.
4. Money market, public expenditure, and federal tax policies aimed at achieving full employment.
5. Policy of steady growth in the money supply to match growth in the economy. No antirecession policies by either the banking system or the federal government. Market adjustment to prevailing economic conditions occurs through decisions made by firm-level management.
6. Work rules and job design jointly determined between employees and management to increase workforce satisfaction and productivity. Works councils.
7. Grievance procedures for arbitrary supervision and enforcement of work rules.
8. Gain-sharing compensation systems where workforce initiated suggestions for use of labor result in higher wage rates and higher profit.

Figure 1.4 (Explanation of Symbols), **continued**

9. Quality circles, advisory to management, where suggested changes in work rules and job design result in higher productivity and profit.
10. Mandated work rules and job design. No formalized grievance procedures.
11. Informally determined work rules under managerial control. No grievance procedures.
12. Union contracts try to slow technological change and specify transfer policies and criteria for layoffs.
13. Works councils jointly determine with management items such as job design, adjustment to technological change, and staffing changes.
14. Featherbedding is used to resist technological change and protect the structural integrity of the union.

---

any one point in time means choosing the proper mix of labor and capital to achieve maximum productivity. For the country as a whole, good utilization of human resources means operating the economy at full employment. Utilization activities become a concern for industrial relations scholars when groups of individuals or their agents negotiate over the means by which maximum productivity and full employment are to be achieved. At the plant level, employees and managers negotiate continuously, though informally, over work effort and the way in which labor and capital are combined. At the national level, labor unions may pressure government to reduce the level of unemployment, to pursue specific kinds of trade and industrial policy, and to influence the rate of technological advance.

Figure 1.4 shows the various activities and negotiations that can occur, again arranged according to the proximity of the negotiation to each center of control. Notice how strongly utilization activities are associated either with management or with government. The utilization of human resources is more closely associated with the overall direction of the firm than any of the other human resource functions. Thus in a free-market system, decisions about utilization will fall heavily to management. In a centrally planned economy, decisions would likewise fall to government. But in neither system is labor likely to achieve total control. At most, labor's influence would be felt through joint labor-management committees or "featherbedding" rules that retain employees even when technological change has undermined their usefulness in the production process. Thus, in figure 1.4, no examples are given for total labor control over the utilization of human resources.

On the far left control axis of figure 1.4, activities generally associated with the term *industrial policy* (the extremes being government control over the entire economic system and full market control) are found. Macro-economic theory provides the arena in which debate over industrial policy occurs. Is monetary policy sufficient to control the path of the economy over time, or are other forms of government intervention necessary to achieve a consistent level of full employment? Given full employment, who will control changes in the employment relationship caused by technological change? Industrial relations scholars tend to be skeptical that full market control will produce an ideal utilization of the workforce. Rather, some form of industrial policy and some type of joint control over the firm's use of labor will be desirable. Industrial relations theorists argue that firm-level control over the utilization of labor does not necessarily restrict productivity and may enhance it (Freeman and Medoff 1984). They also believe that job redesign, works councils, and joint labor-management control over the introduction of new technology could increase job satisfaction and labor productivity. The result is an ever-growing body of theory and research directed at negotiation and labor productivity in business firms.

Human resource utilization activities are the subject matter for much research in an area now known as human resource management (HRM). But the choice of topics to be investigated and the assumptions regarding control can create serious divisions among scholars interested in the traditional topics of unions or collective bargaining and scholars interested in such topics as worker motivation, staffing, and effective management of the workforce. The latter topics may assume that the firm maintains a high degree of control over its workforce. But I argue here that industrial relations scholars reject an assumption of a high level of control either for the firm or for the market. Total firm-level control over the employment relationship should be no more acceptable to a society than total government control, unless the firm serves perfectly as an agent for all its stakeholders: consumers, stockholders, employees, and members of the community in which it operates. Since multiple stakeholders are unlikely to have the same interests, negotiation will occur—preventing full control by either the firm or the market.

Human Resource Maintenance:
Workplace Activities and Related Social Science Theory

Taken in more or less chronological order, human resource maintenance activities are considered last, preceded as they are by development activities that often occur at the beginning of one's work life, allocational activities that occur when first finding a job, and utilization activities that occur continuously over the lifetime of employment. Maintenance activities sustain the employment relationship over time by preserving an employee's skills and health, both while employed and unemployed. Control is reflected on the government side by the degree to which the maintenance function is provided through guaranteed employment (in government-sponsored jobs if necessary) or guaranteed participation in social insurance (unemployment insurance, worker's compensation, social security). On labor and management's side, control is reflected by the degree to which funds are reserved for private pensions, health insurance, and other employee-assistance plans.

Economics is the social science discipline most closely linked to government-sponsored human resource maintenance activities. Economists have examined the effects of receipt of unemployment insurance on the duration of unemployment, calculated the costs of workplace safety regulations, and examined the effects of public pension programs on the national rate of savings and the projected costs of a national system of health insurance. Yet none of this research incorporates the ideas of conflict and negotiation so critical to industrial relations theory. Little of Commons' (1961) framework for analysis of unemployment insurance or the employment service remains in present-day theories or empirical research.

Commons analyzed the philosophies of the various parties who helped propose unemployment insurance legislation in Wisconsin and concluded that an important role existed for collective action and negotiation in first establishing services to job seekers. After determining that some sort of unemployment insurance should be enacted, Wisconsin lawmakers created a state-level advisory committee, which included business representatives opposed to the original unemployment insurance plan. This advisory committee negotiated the final legislative provisions and the plan for administering the program. Bargaining, in this case, allowed a controversial social innovation to occur "without legal compulsion" (Commons 1961, 850). The Commons example demonstrates that if conflict, negotiation, and collective action are to be incorporated into industrial relations theory, strong ties will be needed with political science and sociology, thus de-emphasizing the purely economic side of maintenance activities.

Job seekers often join self-help groups to assist in maintaining themselves during job searches of long duration. To some extent, such self-help groups can serve as agents for job seekers by pooling information on job search tactics and job leads. But their assistance is largely individual—providing emotional support to individual job seekers and trying to place individuals higher on the queues of prospective job applicants. The existence of such groups has not been incorporated into the theory or empirical research on job search. The effectiveness of such groups for maintaining the unemployed during a job search would be a particularly good topic for research. If self-help groups were found to lobby for more job-creation activities, these groups could be treated in the theory developed here as agents who negotiate more favorable positions for all individual job seekers in the market.

A final example of a negotiated resolution to maintenance activities comes from the history of the Social Security Act in the United States. President Roosevelt initially intended that each generation of retirees should pay for its

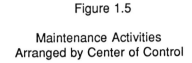

Figure 1.5

Maintenance Activities
Arranged by Center of Control

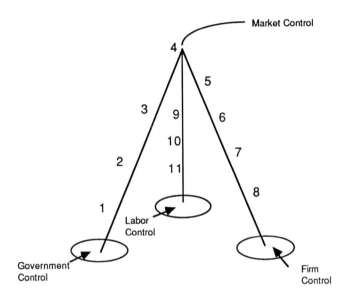

Human Resource Maintenance Activities Shown in Figure 1.5 (Explanation of Symbols)

1. Government-controlled plant committee provides all benefits. Workforce is permanently attached to the firm for life.
2. Government provides social insurance: pensions, unemployment compensation, worker's compensation, and health insurance.
3. Government regulates health and safety, private insurance carriers, and private firms which provide advance notice of layoffs and make adjustments to unfavorable economic conditions. Establishes a minimum wage.
4. Unregulated private firms sell social insurance services to individuals. Companies adjust to economic conditions free of government regulation. No minimum wage.
5. Employee-assistance programs provide information and referrals to employees for health needs and in preparation for layoffs.
6. Private firms sell group social insurance services to company.
7. Company provides its own health services and clinics.
8. Company towns. Multiple services are provided to employees through company owned and operated stores.
9. Union-sponsored job sharing arrangements during recessionary periods.
10. Union-sponsored safety programs.
11. Union-administered health and pension plans.

own retirement by compulsory contribution in advance to a social security trust fund (Stein 1980). The final negotiated solution was a pay-as-you-go system where one generation paid for the previous generation's retirement. The consequence of such a system is that each new generation must negotiate with the next for its own retirement. The baby-boom generation has a tough negotiation ahead of it, but this generation has been preparing for the future by enrolling its members in a strong and politically active institution to represent its interests—the American Association for Retired Persons (AARP). The AARP serves the same purposes as a labor union. The association's bargaining activity, though done through political organizations rather than business firms, can be examined by the same set of theoretical propositions that industrial relations scholars use for other types of negotiation. Private pension plans, privately supplemented unemployment compensation, and job-sharing plans are also negotiated under circumstances that can be better understood through the combined sociological and economic analysis that is familiar ground for industrial relations scholars. At the writing of this book, a comprehensive system of health insurance is being proposed for the United States. The effects of the new system on the employment relationship will undoubtedly be considered, but it is unclear how employers and employees will have their collective interests represented as the plan is presented to Congress. How control over the employment relationship will be affected by this plan is, as yet, unknown.

Summary

A conceptual framework is developed here that directs major attention to the employment relationship. The workplace activities, potential centers for control, and desirable negotiated outcomes depicted in the conceptual framework help to define the field of industrial relations. The field's scope is quite broad. The four categories of workplace activities run the gamut from education and training to social security, and from collective bargaining to a variety of joint labor-management activities. Analysis occurs at several different levels of the economy and theory can be reformist or radical in outlook.

Institutions are critically important. The conceptualization points to four types of institutions: the market, business firms, labor organizations, and government. These institutions may serve as agents for individuals. If so, they become transparent in the theory. In other words, these institutions accurately and consistently represent the interests of their members, are able to resolve their members' inconsistent demands, and have leaders who speak only for members. Institutions other than the market are seen to be in a struggle for control over the employment relationship—acting as agents to protect their members from the intolerable levels of insecurity that can occur due to rapid changes in consumer demands, technology, or costs of production.

In some cases, institutions that have been created to protect members' interests become sources of control themselves. The conceptualization shows how control over the employment relationship can be shifted from total market control to total control by a centrally planned government, for instance. Under monopoly capitalism, control shifts heavily to firms, and in some instances, labor unions may act to preserve their own institutional integrity at the expense of their own members' interests. The theory shows how one institution can serve as a check on another and how the existence of the market can continue to give individuals a choice if institutions garner too much power.

Is there a dynamic at work in the industrial relations system that propels it toward one or another center of control? Marxists argue that this is true and that control over time will accumulate in the hands of a select few—owners of large, monopoly firms. The current downsizing and decentralization of authority in many large firms runs counter to such a prediction, but power and control may not be measured by such trends alone. Will control gradually be subsumed by increasingly authoritarian governments as Heilbroner (1974, 1980) has predicted? The rapid demise of systems of central planning and the rise of democratic forms of governance cast doubt on this possibility, but history also shows that authoritarian systems cannot be easily dismissed. Does the breakdown of communist forms of control over economic life and the internationalism of the world economy mean that the market, in its pure and unregulated form, will emerge as the principle control center for economic activity? Polanyi argues that the economic insecurity of such an arrangement precludes its acceptability over a long period of time even though transitional time periods may impose considerable hardship on the workforce.

The theory developed here suggests another dynamic at work in industrial relations systems. The dynamic starts with the creation of a freely functioning, unregulated market system. In this system, both individuals and firms seek to avoid the pressures of the market. Firms react to the insecurity of the market by growing in size and power and attempting to create relatively stable market environments for themselves. Individuals react to market insecurity by creating agents to negotiate protective rules on their behalf (government agencies or labor unions, for example, and the internal markets of large firms). Agents may also represent individuals in negotiating protection from the control of business enterprises or from excessive governmental power. But as agents grow in influence, they also gain potential for control, thereby extending the dynamic. Individuals may then choose to move policies back in the direction of market control or they may negotiate protection from one agent through another. The dynamic represents a constant movement back and forth between centers of control, with an aim to negotiate an arrangement of shared control.

In this chapter, a mapping out of workplace activities highlights the negotiation dynamic at work and the alternating sources of institutional control that are implicit in each type of activity. In doing so, links to each of the traditional social science disciplines have become clear. The remaining chapters of this book will show in more detail how each of the social sciences contributes to the overall conceptual scheme. Students who specialize in one or another area of human resource activity should be able to see how their own special interests are related to the field as a whole.

Chapter 2

ORIGINS OF THE FIELD
OF INDUSTRIAL RELATIONS

Introduction

The field of industrial relations had its origins in the social scientist's analysis of the industrial revolution. But the industrial revolution has occurred in a variety of contexts and geographical locations. In each, the social and political setting of industrialization shaped the ideas that emerged, a fact reflected in different emphases that academics brought to the four types of workplace activities sketched out in the previous chapter: human resource development, allocation, utilization, and maintenance.

Two sharply opposing schools of thought were a direct outgrowth of the industrial revolution. First was the classical school of economics which placed strong emphasis on free markets and their ability to allocate labor (or any resource or product) efficiently. Second was Marxism which focused on capitalism's power structure and its role in the utilization of labor. Classical economists focused on the benefits that derived from shifting resources from agriculture to industry during the industrial revolution, labor as well as capital; Marxists redirected emphasis away from the efficient allocation of resources and toward a concern for the capitalist's ability to exploit human resources. Classical economists sought an efficient, responsive economic system; Marxists sought a just system.

Two other American schools of thought followed historically and were reactions to the work of Marx and of the classical economists. In this book, these two kinds of American institutionalists will be called "Wisconsin School institutionalists" and "institutional labor economists." In Europe, a similar school of institutional analysis emerged that is generally called pluralism. Wisconsin School institutionalists created an American perspective on labor problems that was clearly intended to compete with the Marxist worldview. These institutionalists focused attention on both the allocation and utilization of labor, and objected to the Marxist concept of class exploitation. Institutional labor economists drew attention to *all* the institutions that affected the employment relationship: training institutions, labor unions, bureaucratic business firms, and government. These labor economists were more interested in debating the ideas of classical economics than they were in engaging Marxism. Their interests spanned all of the workplace activities of my theoretical model. Institutional labor economists described in great detail the actual working of the organizations that were the focus of their attention and showed how the existence of these institutions altered the predictions of classical and neoclassical economists.

European institutional analysis was more apt to deal directly with both power and control. The term *pluralism* derives from the notion that institutions with influence on the employment relationship can, and perhaps should, exist within a rough balance of power (in other words, within a pluralistic system). European pluralists have generally disagreed with Marx's revolutionary predictions, but not with his analysis of the problems of the industrial revolution. Pluralists felt that the labor problem could be resolved in a more evolutionary way with political change the requirement for achieving the desired pluralism of power. The pluralists' perspective contributes significantly to understanding how power affects negotiation over control of the employment relationship.

Classical economists, Marxists, institutionalists, and pluralists all have contributed significantly to various aspects of my conceptual model. In all these traditions, scholars asked what is the labor problem and how should it be resolved? But in one of the most recent schools of thought the labor problem is not nearly as important as a variety of labor problems. Scholars belonging to the human relations school of thought of the mid-twentieth century (or its current successor field, human resource management) have viewed the workplace as one in which many labor problems must be resolved, often through careful firm-level management of individual employees. Kaufman argues that the shift in emphasis from the labor problem to a focus on labor problems has been important for the development of the field of industrial relations because "it recognized that labor problems take many different forms besides labor-management conflict, that labor problems afflict both employers and workers, and that labor problems exist in both socialist and capitalist economies" (Kaufman 1992, 5). Human resource management practitioners and scholars, like the institutionalist labor economists, must deal with all the activities of my conceptual model.

In subsequent chapters of this book, work done by classical economists, Marxists, institutionalists, pluralists, and writers in the area of human resource management is shown—work critical for understanding the dynamics of the model constructed in chapter 1. My task is to clarify the model by way of each of the five traditions. And each, in turn, will help link the traditional social science disciplines with the field of industrial relations. I start by summarizing the various theoretical bases for the model.

Competitive Market Theory

Classical economists examined the origins of industrial society in a market context, placing much emphasis on the allocation of labor. The market was the centerpiece of the theory. These economists analyzed how labor services, like other marketable goods, could be allocated to different uses through adjustments in market price. Eventually, this line of reasoning would link the value of labor services to two main factors: the extra benefit that each additional employee would bring to a business firm and the perceived extra benefit that a job would bring to a potential job holder. Changes in either would result in a reallocation of labor services.

The classical economist's emphasis on allocation was not surprising given the historical context. An important economic concern prior to industrialization in Europe was international trade. Trade was strongly associated with rising national income but, like today, was also strongly affected by the rules of the game. Which would provide more economic benefits to a country—free trade or a system of tariffs? (Presidents of Mexico and leaders of the European Economic Community have in recent years been raising the same questions.) Economists who focus on the efficient allocation of resources argue for free trade and for free-labor markets where labor can move readily from one part of the economic system to another. For the classical economist and for today's neoclassical economists, free-market pricing and the forces of supply and demand are the means to a greater end: economic efficiency and a high rate of economic growth.

Marxism

Karl Marx (1818–1883) initiated his analysis of industrial society before today's familiar concepts of supply and demand had become conventional wisdom. He too wrestled with understanding the value attached to labor, but his approach was quite unlike the approach of the classical economists. Marx raised many of the same questions, but his answers could hardly have been more different. How much should labor be paid? For Marx, workers' wages would ultimately be competed away to subsistence. The value of a worker's production that exceeded subsistence would revert to the owner of capital. Marx argued that most, if not all, of this surplus value should have been paid to labor. As such, surplus value was an implicit measure of capitalist power. Classical economists were less judgmental. For the classical economist, labor should be paid an amount that would employ all those who wanted a job in a particular industry. The value attached to labor was simply a reflection of the value placed by the consumer on the goods and services produced by labor. Labor did not receive the full value of what was produced since the capitalist must receive a competitively determined return on the capital invested. Each individual employee would determine if the wage rate was too low. If it was, the employee could choose not to work or to work in a different industry. The wage rate was not an indicator of injustice in the system. Rather, it showed whether workers were well allocated to jobs where they were needed.

Marx concentrated on how capitalists acquired their labor, and not on how labor was allocated across all possible uses in society. What interested Marx was the process by which labor was bound to the firm over time. The result was Marx's conceptualization of labor as something considerably more than a commodity, or even more than a labor service to be bought and sold in the marketplace.

That Marx emphasized the acquisition of labor and not its allocation is important. Use of the term *acquire* implies a degree of power that classical economists largely ignored. In the classical framework, an impersonal market allocated labor across jobs, as individuals and firms made hard-headed business decisions in response to wage rates. But in the more personal world of Karl Marx, the following industrial relations questions were asked: "Who is acquiring the labor? What is the relationship between the person who acquires the labor and the prospective employee? How much power does each have?" According to Marx, the capitalist acquires the labor. The relationship between capitalist and worker is exploitative. And until the system changes dramatically, the capitalist holds the power.

The schools of thought represented by classical economists and Marxists differed sharply in their analyses of the industrial revolution. But they also differed greatly in methods. Classical economists would ultimately construct a powerful set of theories capable of making precise predictions about human behavior in a world characterized by market transactions and competition. Their methodology was deductive. Still today, neoclassical theory places strong emphasis on prediction and relies on models that specify clearly the causes and effects of economic behavior.

Marxist theory, in contrast, belongs to an academic tradition where knowledge results, in part, from the scholar's own participation in the social system. Participation, in turn, changes both the system and the additional knowledge that can be gained from it (Resnick and Wolff 1987). In Marx's view, revolution was an inevitable prediction for capitalist society, but the blueprint for capitalism's replacement was far from complete. A broad outline of shared ownership and greater equality of earnings could be predicted, but the perfect communist society was less clear than the classical economist's picture of the perfectly competitive market. In part, the ambiguity stemmed from the presumed method of inquiry. The social scientist's participation in the process of change would help to create the new society. A more complete understanding of the new society would accompany the revolutionary changes that preceded the new social system.

The two schools of thought that accompanied the industrial revolution in Europe have led to an enduring fault line in the field of industrial relations. The opposing outlooks represent very different normative evaluations of the industrial revolution and what, if anything, should be done to counter its effects. Classical and neoclassical economists, by emphasizing economic growth and its enhancement through efficient use of resources, have implicitly pointed to the opportunities available in industrial society. Marx and his followers have been much less optimistic, at least in the short run. In their view, efficient growth in a capitalist system has benefited some people at the expense of others. For Marx, the growth in national income was not as important as the growth in power and influence of a tightly knit class of capital owners and the increase in insecurity that the new industrial system imposed on individuals. Only in the long run would new opportunities exist for industrial society—after the capitalist system had been destroyed.

American Institutionalist Thought

The powerful clash of ideas outlined above is a good starting point for understanding three other traditions within the field of industrial relations, each with its own theoretical emphasis. Two of these traditions are North American, each assuming the name institutionalist but quite different in outlook. The third, pluralism, is European. Though also institutionalist in outlook, pluralism has had a much stronger association with political ideology than have either of the North American institutionalist traditions.

In the United States and Canada, industrial society developed under conditions quite different from Europe, resulting in a double reaction to European ideas about industrialization and economic growth. The two academic traditions that embodied these reactions are each referred to as institutionalist; nevertheless, their ideas and the traditions to which they reacted were very different. The U.S. scholar John R. Commons (1862–1945) and his University of Wisconsin students initiated a school of thought that Commons referred to as institutional economics. Commons and his students reacted strongly to Marxist ideas and created a uniquely North American view of the labor problem. A second set of U.S. institutionalists (John Dunlop, Clark Kerr, and Arthur Ross) reacted equally strongly to classical economic theory, arguing that the forces of supply and demand alone were insufficient for understanding the operation of labor markets. These latter institutional economists combined descriptive and historical analyses of labor markets with traditional economic theory to arrive at a more complex theory of human behavior in a market system. As noted above, I refer here to economists and industrial relations scholars who focus attention on the labor market and its associated institutions (labor unions, social insurance, and organizations that provide training) as institutional labor economists. Scholars who focus on the relationship between employees and their managers in industrial enterprises are referred to as Wisconsin School institutionalists. Commons contributed to both of these traditions.

Wisconsin School institutionalists differed from Marx in their identification of the source of industrial conflict. For Marx, the conflict in a capitalistic industrial system stemmed from the social relations of production. In a Marxian world, capital owners, intent on gaining whatever surplus value they could from their workers, set up a system of controls over the workforce that reduced worker autonomy. Workers, by definition, became alienated from the production process because the employment relationship separated them from the means of production and the final output to be sold. Add to this the dissatisfaction that came from low autonomy, technological unemployment, and the instability of an economic system based on ever-growing, monopolistic firms—the result was a formula for revolt. Severe, revolutionary conflict would be inevitable as employment relationships became ever more intolerable.

Wisconsin School institutionalists agreed that conflict was inevitable, but they did not agree with Marx as to either the source or severity of the conflict. For Commons, the problem was not a matter of capitalist ownership or control of the business enterprise. Rather, conflict between labor and management derived from the history and development of markets. If industrial development took place in a system of competitive markets, then worker-controlled firms, government-controlled firms, and capitalist-controlled firms would all experience problems with the inevitable growth of markets. Broader markets were a response to the consumer's demand for standardized, high-quality products in an ever-growing economy (Commons 1913). Mass-produced, high-quality products created demand for a specialized and highly differentiated labor force. The fragmentation of jobs created economic insecurity for the workforce and conflict with management. Unlike the revolutionary conflict predicted by Marx, however, the conflict described by Commons could be dealt with more peacefully—through employment contracts that, among other things, could establish new compensation systems, better working conditions, and job redesign. Government might also help to resolve industrial conflict through social insurance and protective legislation.

Commons and his followers created one set of theories that underlie the framework presented in chapter 1. Wisconsin School institutionalists described in detail the process of negotiation that was at the core of their theory of human behavior. It could be applied equally well to each of the processes outlined—

development, allocation, utilization and maintenance of human resources. But negotiation was assumed to be more indeterminate in its outcome and less amenable to economic modeling than the theory of supply and demand. Commons argued that contracts might result in what he called reasonable value, which could often be determined through the courts or through legislative action and not through the market. Reasonable value applied not only to the monetary determination of wage rates, so critically important for allocating resources, but also to all transactions that were neither "oppressive, confiscatory, or exploitative" (Commons 1961, 672). When, in figure 1.1, individuals—either alone or through the efforts of their agents—negotiate reasonable rules that help to avoid total control over their work lives by any one center of control, these individuals are completing a transaction in Commons' terminology.

The bargaining transactions that Wisconsin School institutionalists envisioned differed greatly from the Marxist's conception of exploitative relationships. Commons and his students agreed that class existed in the United States, but they did not link class with the industrial exploitation of labor. Commons' theory assumed that negotiation could produce protection from the exploitative interests of a particular firm's management. The groups' suggestions for government policy were highly pragmatic and reflected the nonideological stance of the American labor movement. As Barbash has so aptly stated: "Commons sought radical change by conservative means. Government properly employed could play a creative and positive role in alleviating injustice in the workplace, a task that he felt could not safely be left solely to the workings of the market. But reform had to take place within 'the foundations of capitalism': 'I was trying to save capitalism by making it good'" (Barbash 1989, 45).

The historical development of protective institutions to shield individuals from market forces was an important subject both for Wisconsin School institutionalists like Commons and other institutional labor economists. The two schools differed, however, because the Wisconsin School placed considerable emphasis on the protections provided by labor unions, whereas institutional labor economists focused on all of the institutions that contributed to the development of a complex, modern labor market. Many of these institutions protected employees from an oftentimes irregular path of economic development—unemployment insurance, worker's compensation, social security insurance, training institutions, and regional economic development commissions, for example.

The theory used by institutional labor economists was not as elegant as the theory of classical economics, but it was strongly interdisciplinary and historical. Institutionalists dealt explicitly with the tradeoffs in societal values incorporated in labor market institutions—whether worker's compensation should be provided by government or by private firms or whether employers who were in industries characterized by high unemployment should pay the highest tax rates to finance unemployment insurance. In short, institutional labor economists saw the set of rules of the free market as only one of many that could be used to organize production. Constant negotiation would determine which set of rules prevailed and which rules were most reasonable.

As described above, the demarcation between institutional and neoclassical (or classical) economists seems fairly clear. Classical and neoclassical economists have concentrated mainly on the supply side of the market—how and when individuals choose to participate in the labor force, how they gain their education and training and how they search for jobs. Neoclassical labor market analysis has paid less attention to the demand side of the market, assuming that firms were profit seeking and would demand labor through rational calculation of the extra benefit brought to the firm by adding one more person to the payroll. Institutionalists, on the other hand, have argued that the demand for labor might occur in labor markets that were Balkanized (Kerr 1954) or were segmented such that some workers were assigned to the good jobs in the system while others were assigned to the bad (Edwards et al. 1975; Piore 1977). In such a case, attitudes that were institutionalized in the system would arrange people in the job queue with white males at the top and women and minorities at the bottom (Thurow 1972). The job queue, in other words, would not align people according to their potential marginal productivity but rather according to their personal characteristics. These and other institutional characteristics of the market have made demand-side analysis of the market far from straightforward for those who call themselves institutionalists.

Today, the lines separating institutionalists from neoclassical labor economists are growing less clear, due to increasing interest in the theory of implicit contracts. Where institutionalist labor economists left off, neoclassical economists began in their study of implicit contracts. An implicit contract is a set of long-term expectations between employer and employee about the terms of the employment relationship. The implicit contract affects the behavior of both parties and helps to explain some paradoxes in the labor market. Why does long-term employment occur within many firms, despite any legal or collectively bargained requirement for long-term contracts? Why do mandatory retirement provisions exist? Answers to these questions and others have led neoclassical economists into an institutional, demand-side analysis that was not typical of their work before.

At first glance, institutionalist theory seems to place disproportionate emphasis on allocational activities—to the exclusion of the development, utilization, and maintenance activities that are also important in any employment relationship. Yet, if one looks deeper at the key ideas of the institutionalist tradition—reasonable value, implicit contracts, or negotiation—we find that institutionalists have developed theory that cuts across all the processes included in my conceptual framework. Through collective bargaining, reasonable value is strongly associated with the price of labor, and wage rates are particularly important in allocating labor from one potential use to another. But reasonable value can also be established by courts or governmental administrative agencies to affect the maintenance functions of social insurance. Implicit contracts can likewise influence the utilization of labor, and negotiation can help shape the institutions that would educate and protect the workforce over time. In short, North American institutionalist traditions have not really placed a disproportionate emphasis on any one of the human resource activities, emphasizing instead that negotiation among conflicting parties is apt to occur in each.

Fabianism, Nonrevolutionary Socialism, and Pluralism

In Europe, the reaction to Marxist and classical economic theory assumed a different form than in North America. The most vocal challengers were associated with a British academic tradition called Fabian socialism—institutionalist and pragmatic in its outlook, but also ideological. In practice, challengers would create a nonrevolutionary political tradition of democratic socialism to serve as an alternative to Marxist style socialism. This fact alone shows the difference between the largely pragmatic objection to Marx in the United States and the more ideological, political reaction that occurred in Europe.[1]

A brief history of the Fabian Society reveals its academic and political bases. The Fabian Society was founded in Great Britain in 1884 by a group of middle-class intellectuals who wanted a forum to debate socialist ideas. The organization's main purpose was educational, with economist Sidney Webb and sociologist Beatrice Webb two of its most influential leaders. Other leaders were dramatist George Bernard Shaw, future prime minister James Ramsey McDonald, and novelist H. G. Wells.

Though the Fabian Society would never become a political party, the Fabians created the foundation for a reformist political tradition ultimately adopted by many socialist parties in Europe. Two major ideas would be incorporated in the industrial policies espoused by these parties. The first was a belief that the ills of industrial/capitalist society would be lessened by a stronger degree of state control over the means of production. The second was a proposal made by the Webbs (and others) that workers be given more democratic control over the decisions reached by industrial firms. The Fabians believed that a shift of power from concentrated capitalist control to state control and a democratic decentralization of decision making within industrial firms would result in a reformed and more pluralistic industrial society. In the Fabians' view, industrial democracy would strengthen political democracy.

For the Webbs, the labor union was an important reformist institution for creating a more equitable society. Marx also considered unions to be reformist, but they served an ambiguous role in his theoretical framework. On the one hand, the union could ameliorate the effects of a harmful employment relationship between capitalists and workers. On the other hand, union activities would delay the inevitable overturn of a highly undesirable social system and its progression toward utopia. The Webbs did not view the labor union ambiguously; nor did they believe in the inevitability of revolution. The Webbs argued, instead, that reform could occur through the democratization of industrial enterprises that accompanies unionization. They based these beliefs on an exhaustive analysis of labor unions in nineteenth-century Great Britain (Webb and Webb 1897).

The reaction to Marxism in Britain resulted in an academic tradition among British industrial relations scholars called pluralism. Pluralists espouse a philosophy that is in many ways similar to Wisconsin School institutionalists. In both traditions, free collective bargaining is a means for achieving pragmatic economic gains for individual workers. And in both traditions, the existence of labor unions means that the bases of power within industrial society are diversified. Scholars in each tradition have argued that in a pluralist industrial society a balance of power exists between management and labor, with government serving as arbiter.

British writers who adopt more Marxist views of industrial power have challenged the notion of pluralism. Fox, for example, argues that the current balance of power in collective bargaining overlooks the right that management has to close plants, shift product lines, and internationalize production (Fox 1973). The power to make such critical decisions within the firm dwarfs the collective bargaining relationship that deals mainly with wages and working conditions.

European scholars have, in effect, turned attention to two of the alternative centers of control discussed in chapter 1. Control can be with government—a political control in which ideology plays an important role. Or control can be at the firm level—shared among many competitive firms or a few monopolistic firms. In all cases, pluralism argues against a system in which the government or the firm retains the vast majority of power. Relationships among labor, management, and government are to be negotiated, resulting in a broad sharing of power and control.

Human Resource Management

The fifth and final academic tradition that has influenced the field of industrial relations has done so by way of its profound impact on the practice of management. In 1911, an American engineer, Frederick W. Taylor, published the *Principles of Scientific Management* in which he outlined a series of reforms for the organization of work in industrial firms. Taylor's efficiency studies led to a series of reactions and counterreactions that culminated in the establishment of personnel departments within modern business firms. Taylor's school of scientific management and subsequent reactions to it (for example, the human relations movement) were to have important implications, both for industrial workplace relationships and for industrial relations thought.

In the early part of this century, industrial relations scholars focused their attention on the labor problem and the influence that the institutions of government and labor can have on it. The more recent human resources tradition, in contrast, stresses the influence that a problem-centered management can have on its workforce and/or its labor union. The tradition has assumed different names over time. Early scholars in this tradition were either associated with the school of scientific management or its counterpoint, the human relations movement. As major corporations developed specialized personnel departments, universities in turn initiated programs in personnel management. In more recent years, the same general subject area has been called human resource planning, human resource administration, and strategic human resource management.

Many institutionalists and Marxists alike tend to be uncomfortable with the individualistic assumptions of the human resource tradition. Human resource management directs its attention at individual compensation schemes, an individual's career development, individualized training programs, and the recruitment, selection, and placement of individuals within work organizations. The institutional nature of the workplace is de-emphasized. It is often assumed that the human resource department can generally serve the best interests of the firm's employees. Marxists and institutionalists, to differing degrees, are skeptical that the firm will always serve the interests of employees. Both believe that some degree of conflict of interest will exist.

Marxists, in particular, disagree with the assumptions of human resource management. Marxists (and others as well) argue that the term *human resource* itself implies that employees are to be used for managerial purposes. Students of human resource management, on the other hand, tend to view the term in a more neutral way. They assume that in many areas, the interests of employees and their managers will coincide and, if so, managerial exploitation is not an issue.

The analysis of how an individual's abilities and skills could be best used to further the business enterprise's goals was characteristic of the school of thought known as scientific management. Although this school of thought originated as an engineering approach to the organization of work, the success of the program rested on the willingness of individual workers to accept the incentive pay plans proposed by Frederick R. Taylor, the school's founder and enthusiastic spokesperson for scientific management. Proponents of scientific management assumed that workers were motivated by pay and would be satisfied with whatever share of productivity improvement management might award to labor (Taylor 1911).

In retrospect, the engineering innovations accomplished by Taylor and his associates were successful, but Taylor's expectations for individual behavior were not always borne out. Workers resisted the establishment of piece-rate systems, especially after recognizing that rates could be adjusted once productivity improved. The power of management to establish rates was not well incorporated into the social scheme envisioned by scientific management, and the power of the work group to enforce its own norms on individuals was underestimated (Aitken 1960).

The effects of work groups on individuals in the workplace was addressed by the school of human relations, popularized by Elton Mayo. Beginning with a series of experiments performed at Western Electric, Mayo proposed a philosophy of management that differed sharply from the school of scientific management (Roethlisberger and Dickson 1939; Mayo 1945). The school of human relations recognized the relatively complex social setting of the business firm—one in which work groups influenced individual work effort.

Subsequent to Mayo, researchers who adopted an individual perspective in studying industrial relations focused on motivation, rewards, and how some individuals could shape the behavior of others through the structuring of those rewards. The human resource management tradition that followed both Mayo and Taylor has emphasized the development of human resources, the allocation of these resources through systems of human resource planning, and the maintenance of skills over time. Although Taylor's scientific management tended to focus unduly on the utilization process, the broader human resource tradition has given a more balanced emphasis to each of the four key activities included in my theoretical framework.

Institutionalists, Marxists, and human resource management scholars alike have occupied important places within the development of industrial relations thought. As a consequence, the field openly invites debate. But the debate is often difficult to resolve since it rests on values, assumptions, and theoretical emphases, not solely on empirical verification of a commonly accepted set of theoretical propositions. The result is tension, conflict, and sometimes antagonism within the field, perhaps a reflection of the same forces at work within industrial society.

Summary

The five schools of thought outlined in this chapter have had a profound impact on the policies of a variety of industrialized countries. Underlying each school of thought is at least one of the social science disciplines of economics, political science, psychology, and sociology. History and the law are also important for understanding the dynamics of industrial relations policies. In four of the traditions (Marxism, the two forms of American institutionalism, and pluralism), the institutions of society are the focus of the analysis, not the individual worker. In neoclassical labor economics and in the area of human resource management, the predominant emphasis is on the individual. In the chapters that follow, all five traditions will be examined in more detail. For each, the model described in chapter 1 will be used to show how both individual behavior and institutions are important to help bridge the differences in the traditions and to connect each to a wide variety of social science theories.

Chapter 3

MARXISM, ECONOMICS, AND
INDUSTRIAL RELATIONS

Today's Marxists and non-Marxists alike owe much to the man whose name gives both groups identity. And for industrial relations scholars, Karl Marx's legacy is particularly great. Few would question the influence of Marx on the debate over the future direction of capitalist, industrial society—toward revolution or a much less cataclysmic process of change. But Marx's influence is perhaps most important in analyzing very personal relationships of people at work.

Karl Marx and the Employment Relationship

In this book, the employment relationship is assumed to be central to industrial relations theory; it is also central to the Marxist theory of capitalist production. For Marx, a work role is comprised of a set of relationships among people at work, what he referred to as the social relations of production: "In production, men not only act on nature but also on one another. They produce only by co-operating in a certain way and mutually exchanging their activities. In order to produce, they enter into definite connections and relations with one another and only within these social connections and relations does their action on nature, does production, take place" (Tucker 1978, 207).

Roles do not exist in isolation but rather in a web of other societal relationships. Marx believed that through careful description of all of society's relationships, workplace analysis could be linked to predictions about the future direction of capitalist society. Perhaps, then, the entire industrial system should be viewed as a web of rules which, if shaped or reshaped, would change workplace relationships as a result (Dunlop 1958). Dunlop's web image is not Marxist, however. For a Marxist, the web of rules does not shape work roles; rather, the work roles that exist under capitalist production shape all the other relationships in society. The industrial relations system is not greater than the sum of its parts. It does not shape or change work-role relationships—it is derived from them: "The sum total of these relations of production constitutes the economic structure of society, the real foundation, on which rises a legal and political superstructure and to which correspond definite forms of social consciousness. The mode of production of material life conditions the social, political and intellectual life process in general" (Tucker 1978, 4).

Marxist thinking challenges the beliefs of liberal political activists the world over. If one wants a more democratic workplace, can one not achieve it by an appropriate mix of government legislation and collectively bargained contracts? Does not governmental social policy change the economic and social structure of the system in which all people live and work? Marx's answer is: No, it does not. The most basic outlines of the system are predetermined by the predictable work roles and relationships that exist under capitalism. Only under special historical circumstances can these relationships be expected to change, and when they do change, the result will be revolution.

Marxism and Political Economy

The history of the field of industrial relations is one of reactions and counterreactions. Marx reacted strongly to the writings of the economists of his day, and other industrial relations scholars, in turn, reacted to him. Marx derided students of political economy because they emphasized prices to the neglect of other important dynamics of the economic system. The counterargument of the economists of Marx's day and today is that prices help to resolve important technical relationships of production. Managers are assumed to make choices about the kinds of production processes to use—some of which will require more capital machinery and some of which will require less. In today's economic language, managers make choices after considering the full set of technical options for combining labor and capital in the production process—these managers make choices based on the firm's production function.

For Marx, the most important relationships of production were social, not technical. Instead of focusing on the technical production function, Marx emphasized the relationships between workers and their bosses. In Marx's view, even the machinery of production embodied social relationships since the money to purchase it was obtained through a unique set of social exchanges or transactions. According to Marx, "capital also is a social relation of production" (Tucker 1978, 207). He elaborates as follows:

All combined labour on a large scale requires, more or less, a directing authority. . . . The work of directing, superintending, and adjusting, becomes one of the functions of capital, from the moment that the labour under the control of capital, becomes co-operative. . . . The directing motive, the end and aim of capitalist production, is to extract the greatest possible amount of surplus-value, and consequently to exploit labour-power to the greatest possible extent. (Tucker 1978, 385)

When analyzing the employment relationship, Marx saw exploitation. He made two strong and unequivocal value judgments. Workers have an inherent right to a portion of the value of the product or service that they help to create, and these workers should lay claim to more than is necessary for them to subsist. Yet under capitalism, the owners of capital extract all value produced in excess of the amount necessary to keep a worker alive. The result is the increased well-being of the bourgeoisie at the expense of the proletariat. "The control exercised by the capitalist is . . . rooted in the unavoidable antagonism between the exploiter and the living and labouring raw material he exploits" (Tucker 1978, 385).

In the Marxian world (or in any other, for that matter), who determines the expectations that help to define work roles? For the economist, work roles are viewed technically—various combinations of labor and capital as spelled out by a production function. Production technology, once chosen, defines work roles for those who must operate the machinery of production. Marx sought to amplify the economists' analysis by asking who defines work roles and for what purpose. A work role could be defined by someone in authority. It could also be defined by coworkers. Marx focused attention on those in authority—members of the ruling class—who define work roles for everyone else. Marx posited that the bourgeoisie construct roles so that maximum surplus value can be extracted from the proletariat.

Class Structure as the Entry Point
to Marxist Analysis

For Marx, technology is neither an unimportant factor in determining work roles nor is the influence of coworkers. In fact, it is hard to pinpoint just who or what is ultimately responsible for capitalist relationships of production since work-role relationships are determined more or less simultaneously with other societal processes. Resnick and Wolff refer to this aspect of Marxist theory as over determination. Since everything determines everything else, "Marxian theory has a starting point, but the theory never ends in the sense of a 'complete' social analysis. . . . Marxian theory is open; it never completes its formulation of the social totality" (Resnick and Wolff 1987, 25).

Class is, however, the entry point of Marxist theory—"the economic process of performing and appropriating surplus labor" (Resnick and Wolff 1987, 26). By linking all other processes to the class process of appropriating surplus value, Marx maintains a unity in his outlook on the world, but at the risk of serious damage to the theory if the entry point is flawed. In the capitalist system, Marx claimed that the ruling classes appropriated surplus value from labor thereby maintaining their position of power within the system. The historical tendency of technology to create an increasing division of labor (simplifying tasks) reduced workers' power within capitalist firms because they could easily be replaced. Furthermore, Marx assumed that technological change would lead to an ever-growing mass of workers who were thrown out of work. The result was an impending crisis in which employed workers would realize their tentative position within the firm and join with the unemployed to change the entire system of production.

A Comparison of Marxist and Non-Marxist
Industrial Relations Theorists

The work role is central to Marxist theory, but the role is one that is prescribed for employees by capitalist authority (or class). For Marxists, the production relationships that accompany capitalist work roles lead inevitably to crisis and a revolutionary change in the system. For non-Marxists, the work role is also central to industrial relations theory, but both the presupposition that surplus value belongs to the workers and the prediction that the capitalist system will self-destruct are open to question. Not surprisingly, non-Marxists focus their objections to Marxist thought on the entry point to the theory—the class process. If class relationships are more complex than depicted by Marx, then the impetus for change in the system (conflict between the proletariat and the bourgeoisie) may never come about. The different emphases of Marxists and non-Marxists can be seen by taking a closer look at the conceptual model presented in chapter 1, thus permitting a sharper comparison between the two schools of thought.

The model describes the employment relationship in terms of four main activities: the development, allocation, utilization, and maintenance of human resources. Marxists and non-Marxists place different emphasis on the importance of each of these activities, however. The negotiation of control over each of the activities is viewed differently between Marxists and non-Marxists, as well as the amount of conflict that will occur over time.

Marx placed his greatest emphasis on the process of human resource utilization, whereas classical economists placed the most emphasis on allocation. For Marx, the capitalist system permitted a class of property owners to use human resources to maintain themselves (the owners) in power. Human resources were maintained at subsistence level while the power of the capitalist class was maintained via an exploitive relationship with the working class. As shown in the model presented in chapter 1, the utilization of labor would be controlled unilaterally by management, with no grievance channels for addressing work rules or job design (specific activities ten and eleven in the model).

Marx paid little or no attention to the development process, at least as it referred to the workforce itself. Marx predicted how the entire economic system would develop over time but not how human resources might be developed. He envisioned no incentive for capitalists to develop the human resources of workers since technological change and the interests of capitalists themselves would push the economic system toward greater and greater division of labor. Furthermore, the control of the capitalist class over other societal institutions would also constrain individuals in developing their own human resources. Little incentive would exist for government to subsidize worker training through educational grants and loans given the strong connection between government and the interests of the ruling class.

Marxist theory places emphasis on the utilization process, but due to the influence of class, certain utilization activities are more likely to characterize work roles than others. In terms of this model, Marx placed the greatest emphasis on the specific activities that occurred when employers had a great deal of control over utilization, namely through the establishment of work rules and through job design. Job design enhanced the power of the capitalist class, according to Marx, because tasks could be simplified as the capitalist system developed over time. Division of labor eroded whatever power individual workers may have had by stripping them of marketable skills and making them ever more vulnerable to layoff. Eventually the insecurity that employed workers felt in the presence of a competitive market was almost as great as the insecurity felt by unemployed workers and thereby facilitated a joining of their interests in opposing the capitalist class.

A further result of the division of labor was a sense of alienation within the working class:

> What, then, constitutes the alienation of labour? First, the fact that labour is external to the worker, in other words it does not belong to his essential being; that in his work, therefore, he does not affirm himself but denies himself, does not feel content but unhappy, does not develop freely his physical and mental energy but mortifies his body and ruins his mind. The worker therefore only feels himself outside his work, and in his work feels outside himself. He is at home when he is not working, and when he is working he is not at home. His labour is therefore not voluntary, but coerced; it is forced labour. It is therefore not the satisfaction of a need; it is merely a means to satisfy needs external to it. . . . Lastly, the external character of labour for the worker appears in the fact that it is not his own,

but someone else's, that it does not belong to him, that in it he belongs, not to himself, but to another. (Tucker 1978, 74)

Alienation occurs because work is a means to an end. Work results in self-denial, rather than self-affirmation, because in the end the capitalist owns all the means of production, including work itself.

Marxist Predictions of Change in the Employment Relationship Over Time

Marxist theory predicts a particular kind of development of the entire capitalist system as it ages. The historical development of capitalism, in turn, leads to changes in the way work roles are defined, changes that can also be identified in this model. Marx predicted that the capitalist system would move from competitive to monopoly capitalism and from monopoly capitalism to socialism, but how would the employment relationship be affected? The shift from competitive to monopoly capitalism would increase the exploitation of the workforce as the number of unemployed workers grew larger. The system would collapse in revolution and be replaced by a socialist state with public ownership of all property. The manner in which labor power was employed would change from activities characterized by a high degree of control by firms (numbers ten and eleven in the model) to activities in which government was in control (numbers one and two).

In the socialist state, government would at least in theory serve as an agent for the worker, converting the exploitive activities of private property owners to activities in which workers and government central planners would share in decisions about the utilization of labor. The planned socialist system would remedy the original lack of maintenance activities in the capitalist system by introducing a variety of health and welfare activities provided by an employee's work unit. In the real world, government has not always acted as an agent for workers. If the revolutionary process does not guarantee that the government will continue to be accountable to the workforce, control may quickly shift from a locus centered on the firm to one centered on government. Work-role activities become those where again individual workers have little influence or control. The Marxist assumption of strong class antagonism serves to justify the dramatic change in control that occurs when centrally planned socialism replaces monopoly capitalism. If central planning completely replaces the market, individuals may have little influence over the newly empowered group of planners. If, on the other hand, some degree of market control is preserved or reintroduced, workers may then be able to negotiate for a new set of activities that represents shared control between individuals and the government. Centralized government control over investment decisions (activity number one) could yield to indirect control through money market, public expenditure, and tax policies (activity number four)—giving individuals much more leeway to negotiate their preferred place in the economic system. In China today, these kinds of experiments are referred to as market reforms.

Marx Compared with Classical Economists

A classical economist's view of the world differs greatly from Marx. Marx focused attention on the processes of utilization and maintenance, de-emphasizing the processes of allocation and development. Classical economists did just the opposite, emphasizing the processes of allocation and development, and downplaying utilization and maintenance. The political economists whom Marx derided argued that a process of exchange existed between workers and employers, not exploitation. In their view, if capitalism were accompanied by free markets, the relationship between capitalists and workers would be exploitive only for monopolies. The market would prevent exploitation by pitting one employer against another, thereby reducing each one's power relative to the worker.

In the classical economists' view, the process of class conflict would not interact with other work-role processes since competition and free markets would divide the interests of individual capitalists. Class differences might still characterize society since income differences could readily be converted to class differences through income expenditures. But class differences would not be derived solely from exploitive work-role relationships. A variety of work-role relationships would be determined by the choice of efficient technology, adopted under competitive market conditions. Where employee skills were low and their market power weak, labor might appear to be exploited. Nevertheless, pay would still be established through a voluntary exchange as markets and competition determined the wage rates that individuals were willing to accept for their labor services. Surplus value would not exist.

In the last two hundred years, economists have devoted much attention to the allocative mechanisms of the market economy, spelling out in elaborate detail the calculations of costs and benefits that underlie the forces of supply and demand. But have they really downplayed the utilization of labor as argued above? From an economist's perspective, the utilization of labor is understood through reference to the firm's production function, namely all the combinations of labor and capital that are required to produce a full range of output. Economists have neither neglected the theoretical conceptualization of the production function nor its empirical specification. But the field of economics does assume that if resources have been allocated efficiently, their utilization in production will be no great mystery. Given the prices of labor and capital, efficient combinations will be obvious to the owners of a business enterprise. The process of allocating resources is therefore considerably more important than utilization.

The second important area in which classical economists differed from Marx is in the emphasis placed on the process of development. For Marx, the fortunes of individual workers were inextricably tied to the development of the entire capitalist system. The development of skills which could make work more meaningful would be impossible on two counts. First, the advance of technological change under the direction and control of capitalists would result in a division of labor, or what neo-Marxists would eventually define as a process of "deskilling" (Braverman 1974). "The more productive capital grows, the more the division of labour and the application of machinery expands. The more the division of labour and the application of machinery expands, the more competition among the workers expands and the more their wages contract" (Tucker 1978, 216).

This, coupled with an ever-growing population, would drive wages to subsistence, thereby yielding no excess funds for workers to invest in their own education and training: "When political economy claims that demand and supply always balance each other, it immediately forgets that according to its own claim (theory of population) the supply of people always exceeds the demand" (Tucker 1978, 100).

A view that collides sharply with the above Marxist argument has in more recent years been called the human capital school of economic thought. The set of arguments proposed by human capital theorists in the 1950s and 1960s is not really new, however. The ideas were well anticipated by classical economists like Adam Smith (1776). The non-Marxist argument of Adam Smith and recent human capital economists (Becker 1962, 1975; Mincer 1958, 1962) is as follows: as an economy develops, employees begin to gain useful skills simply by working a sufficiently long time with the machinery of production. A market will develop for work experience since it is often useful in other firms. Among firms, competition for talent drives up the wages of skilled workers and converts employees, at least in part, to capitalists. Workers who now own their human capital can rent it to the highest bidder, thereby obtaining wages higher than subsistence. Alternatively, employees may borrow or be granted sufficient funds to invest in their own training if future earnings are sufficiently high to convince them to undertake the risks of investment. Again, workers, in part, become capitalists. (This is true if at least some significant portion of training is general and can be marketed to a variety of employers. If all training is firm-specific and therefore offered only by the employer, the employee would have no opportunity to acquire independent power by marketing skills to competitors.)

Marx's counterargument to the classical economists was that the division of labor would negate the possibilities for workers to become capitalists. But if valuable skills indeed are developed by individual workers, the interests of the working class will be considerably less homogeneous than Marx assumed. Therefore, the debate between Marxists and non-Marxists over the influence of economic development and technological change is directly related to the debate over class interests and power.

In the final analysis, Marxist thought differs most strongly from classical economics in its assumptions about power relationships. Classical economists were able to ignore any imbalance in power relationships through an assumption of perfect competition. Therefore, they could stress the importance of resource allocation in the work-role environment. Managers were simply responding to the technical necessity of combining resources efficiently when they sought to enter into exchanges with workers. Marx, in contrast, predicted the demise of purely competitive capitalism and its replacement by large-scale monopolies.

Under a system of monopoly capitalism, the power relationship at the workplace would be highly imbalanced. Because of the division of labor and an expanding population, capitalists would obtain surplus value from the workforce, thereby reinforcing the power of the capitalists as a class. Marx assumed there was an imbalance of power that led to a transfer of surplus value from workers to capitalists. For classical economists, competition among firms eliminated the possibility for surplus value—leaving in its place a process of exchange. The value exchanged for work had to be higher than the value employees attached to nonwork. In addition, the exchange had to compensate for previous investments in human capital. For Marx, class power was a totally expected part of the relationship between workers and managers. For classical economists, class power could be part of the broader social system, but it was irrelevant to the relationships between managers and workers. There, the competitive process of exchange restricted the power of managers vis-à-vis their employees.

Classical economists side-stepped questions about power in society because they disagreed with Marx that monopoly capitalism would inevitably replace competitive capitalism. In addition, they disagreed that work-role relationships would determine all the other relationships of society. Classical economists would have agreed with modern-day social activists that work roles and shop-floor power relationships can be changed by appropriate government policy. Adam Smith, for example, argued that mercantilist trade policies should and could be changed simply by removing restrictions on trade, thereby allowing free markets to operate unhampered by government regulation. By fostering competitive forces, classical economists believed that the power of central government and of monopoly business firms could be limited. Students of the perfectly competitive system would henceforth examine power relationships only as exceptions to the general model. Furthermore, the solution for imbalanced power relationships was simple—create a more competitive market.

Summary

A comparison of the theories of classical Marxists with classical economists yields two internally consistent but strikingly different worldviews. Despite their internal consistency, however, neither may be an accurate depiction of the employment relationship as it actually exists. In my conceptual framework, negotiation is very much a part of employment relationships—negotiation to prevent too much control falling to the market, the business firm, the government, or a labor organization. Neither classical economists nor Marxists see much of a role for negotiation in determining how labor is to be utilized.

Classical economists assume that work rules and roles are not negotiated but rather are mandated by the adoption of the most efficient technology within the firm. The market is an unforgiving taskmaster, rewarding those who adopt the most efficient production processes and forcing out of business those who do not. The authority structure of the industrial firm is designed to arrive at the most efficient solutions to production problems.

Marxists also assume that work rules and roles are mandated, but the market is not the driving force. Rather, class interests and the need for control over the workforce dictate how work roles will be defined. Although some negotiation over work roles may occur, the ultimate power within the system is clear. The interests of the ruling class drive the system forward in time.

Industrial relations scholars, unlike the Marxists or the classical economists, assume that work rules and roles are negotiated and not mandated. A variety of work rules can be negotiated to regulate how labor is used in the enterprise. In fact, even the authority structure of the firm itself can be negotiated through demands for participative management. Still, the world is quite unpredictable from the perspective of an industrial relations scholar whose theory is based neither on Marx nor on neoclassical economics. Much is negotiable, and the outcome is hard to predict. A knowledge of markets and how they function will narrow the range of unpredictability since markets set the boundaries for negotiations and dictate the limits within which efficient use of resources must occur. Similarly, an understanding of institutions, their sources of power, and their objectives can yield insight into the nature of negotiation, thereby increasing predictability. Finally, a better understanding of the determinants of individual motivation, attitudes, and behavior can clarify when and how individuals will act alone or through institutions to influence employment relationships. Such knowledge can only be obtained by reference to virtually all of the social science disciplines. A survey of those areas within the social sciences that are most important for understanding the employment relationship is the main task of each of the chapters that follow. In several of them, the influence of Marx and of neoclassical economics will continue to be seen, setting the terms for lively debate.

Chapter 4

Social Systems, Conflict, and Change

Kaufman pointed out that at its inception in the 1920s, industrial relations had a very broad disciplinary base—encompassing ideas from anthropology, psychology, social psychology, sociology, economics, ethics, and education (Kaufman 1993, chap. 1). Today, these fields seem quite distinct, but it was not always so. Sociology, for example, was only beginning to gain legitimacy as an academic department separate from economics and psychology in the early twentieth century. The American Economic Association had been founded in 1885 and the American Psychological Association in 1892, but the American Sociological Association was not founded until 1903 (Waldo 1976, 34). Political science followed a similar pattern, with the first department separate from economics established at Columbia University in 1880 (Waldo 1976, 26). The American Political Science Association was established in 1903. Industrial relations was first established as a separate academic unit when a special section was created in Princeton's Economics Department in 1922 (Kaufman 1993, chap. 1). In this chapter, I discuss sociology, political science, and industrial relations together, minimizing the differences that have grown among them. (Economics and psychology will be dealt with separately.) In this sense I try to capture at least some portion of the spirit that characterized the field of industrial relations in the early part of this century. Systems theory serves as a starting point for showing how each of these seemingly separate areas are interrelated.

As the social sciences and industrial relations sought to establish their own separate identities, debate occurred over the theoretical paradigm that would be used to study each area's own special concerns. Competing theories, in many cases, helped to establish the identity of each field—the neoclassical tradition versus institutional theory within economics, cognitive versus behavioral theories in psychology, and systems theory versus a less structured worldview in sociology and political science. But the theories also retained connections to each other across the disciplines—a fact that becomes quite apparent when relating these theories to industrial relations.

In several of the social sciences, important debate has occurred over systems theory, a topic that is important since most industrial relations scholars assume that employment relationships are part of a broader social system. Here I review the theories of sociologists and political scientists who support this underlying assumption and contrast their view with those who are in dissent. Secondly, I look to both fields for the tools to understand how institutions are formed, how they shape behavior, and how they can encourage both coopera- tion and conflict in the workplace. Finally, I ask what either of the two fields can contribute to an understanding of the role of negotiation in the employment relationship.

The Sociological Debate Over Systems Theory

One of the more central debates in both sociology and political science is whether an all encompassing social system exists, a debate that is important here since the model discussed in chapter 1 clearly assumes a social system. Labor, management, and government are actors in the system and negotiate rules, not only for the workplace, but also on their own behalf. The institutions of labor, management and government may or may not act exclusively as agents for the individuals they represent. As actors, they build a social system that is, at least to some degree, self-perpetuating.

The systems view of the world is often credited to the work of the sociologist, Talcott Parsons. The term *systems theory* is derived from Parsons' conception of a social system with identifiable actors and a tendency toward equilibrium. This view of society would ultimately be applied by John Dunlop to the industrial relations practices of specific countries—in other words, their industrial relations systems. Predating Parsons, however, was the quite differ- ent systems theory of Karl Marx. For Marx, an elaborate economic and social system existed, but it was a system that was not characterized by equilibrium. Instead, the actions of groups of individuals (or classes) drove the system for- ward in time and closer to a period of revolutionary change.

Any social system has actors—groups of people who act as one. In the Marxist system, there were only two main actors: workers and capitalists (the proletariat and the bourgeoisie). The actors were not real people, however; they were constructs of the mind. For convenience the people were treated as if they were real—their actions and motives were analyzed and predicted. Any sys- tems theorist argues that by constructing actors, one can understand individual behavior better than if the collection of behaviors of a diverse population is analyzed. If one accepts the systems theorist's viewpoint, society becomes an independent level of reality.

Functionalism and the Debate Over Marxist Theory

Within sociology, early debate about Marxist theory was not so much whether a social system existed but rather a debate over the functions played by people in the system and how these functions changed over time. Marx's outlook was quite functionalist. Capitalists and workers had very functional roles to play in society, and as they played out these functions, their actions inevitably led to the system's demise. Max Weber (1864–1920), Emile Durkheim (1858–1917), and Talcott Parsons (1902–1979) were also functionalists, but they had a much less rigid view of how the functions of various actors would relate to change in the system over time.

Weber, Durkheim, and Parsons argued that positions in society are ranked in value first according to their importance to society as a whole, and secondly according to the scarcity of people available to fill the positions. Most modern-day economists are in fact functionalists. According to conventional economic theory, the preferences of consumers (society) are reflected in the wages paid to employees who produce the goods and services consumers want—the demand side of the market. From the wages paid, one can (and does) rank order the jobs chosen. But wages are also a function of the number of people willing to work in particular occupations—the supply side of the market. The combination of demand and supply results in a ranking of the positions of society by occupation—with some occupations being paid much more than others. Marx, in contrast, argues that positions in society are ranked according to a single criterion—ownership of capital. Those who own the most capital receive the most income, power, and prestige in society; those who own the least capital receive the least income and other benefits. Most modern-day sociologists and economists argue that the ranking of jobs in society results in a whole series of classes or strata of differing income and social prestige based on occupation. For a Marxist, though, the only meaningful societal divisions are between the capital owners (the bourgeoisie) and those who work for them (the proletariat).

Max Weber

Max Weber argued that classes or strata in society developed because of the actions of specific individuals in defense of their own interests. He defined closure to mean the process by which "social collectivities seek to maximize rewards by restricting access to resources and opportunities to a limited circle of eligibles" (Parkin 1979, 44). Such closure would lead to divisions or stratifications within society. Weber argued that divisions in society can occur for reasons other than the ownership of capital. Note, however, that while Weber objected to the type of system outlined by Marx, he still retained a systems view of the world. Weber thought of society as a system that both constrained and shaped individual human behavior.

A systems theorist focuses on the relationships among the actors in the system, and for Weber, this meant asking how classes were related to each other at various points in time. Parkin summarizes what he calls the neo-Weberian view of the relationship among classes as follows:

The neo-Weberian position . . . is that the relation between classes is neither one of harmony and mutual benefit, nor of irresolvable and fatal contradiction. Rather, the relationship is understood as one of mutual antagonism and permanent tension; that is, a condition of unrelieved distributive struggle that is not necessarily impossible to 'contain.' Class conflict may be without cease, but it is not inevitably fought to a conclusion. The competing notions of harmony, contradiction, and tension could thus be thought of as the three broad possible ways of conceptualizing the relation between classes, and on which all class models are grounded. (Parkin 1979, 112)

The so-called neo-Weberian view of the world is one held by many industrial relations and human resource management practitioners in the business world today. The workplace is characterized by permanent tension but it can be managed or at least contained. At various points in time, a workplace can be characterized by harmony, contradiction, or tension. The divisions within the work society are real and thus harmony or mutual benefit cannot always be assumed, but neither is it assumed that the problems that arise are irreconcilable.

Weber still conceived of society as a system with various actors (classes), but he differed from other systems theorists (Marx in particular) in the way in which he presumed that the actors in the system would relate to one another. The relationship was one of reconcilable conflict.

Emile Durkheim

The French sociologist and functionalist, Durkheim, argued persuasively that society should be viewed as an independent level of reality, though he likewise did not accept the Marxist presumption that it was fraught with irreconcilable contradictions (Smelser 1988, 10). Instead, he focused on the integration of society by the functional roles assigned to members of the system. By the 1950s, Durkheim's view had become the relatively predominant one in the field of sociology. Reflecting back on that period of time, Smelser comments on what he sees as the three ways in which a Durkheimian vision of sociology had risen to prominence:

The first was that sociology is the study of observable and objective *facts* in the social world—not speculative philosophy, nor moral inquiry. . . . The second respect was the Durkheimian insistence that sociological investigation lies at an analytically distinct *social*—not psychological or biological—level, and that society constitutes an independent level of reality . . . and the third element . . . was that with regard to the understanding of social systems, greatest stress was given to the functional coherence and integration of their component parts. (Smelser 1988, 10)

Managers seeking to devise cooperative, relatively conflict-free workplaces would undoubtedly support Durkheim's position that if one wants to understand the social system of work in an organization, one should give the greatest stress to the various functions of the organization and how they are to be integrated into coordinated economic activity. Management researchers who develop theory to explain the behavior of individuals in complex organizations (scholars in the field of organizational behavior) have been strongly influenced by Durkheim's view of society. A review of recent organizational behavior research in the most important industrial relations journals reveals a strong emphasis on the functions of the organization and the role of the organization in resolving conflict, coordinating activity, and integrating individuals into a corporate culture.

The structural functions of economic organizations—both business firms and labor unions—are stressed in two important areas of organizational behavior reseach: the organization's structure and its overall effectiveness. Researchers and practitioners have long been interested in the outcomes of centralized and decentralized bargaining structures (Ready 1990; Brauer 1990). But Durkeim's view is most evident in studies that link organizational structure with employee or union participation in managerial decision making. Wever (1989), for example, distinguished between structural effects on participation (those relating to power) from cognitive effects (those relating to perceptions). Her view of organizations was very much the same as Durkheim's: "[My] premise is that the structural basis of the union-management relationship shapes both the cognitive understandings and attitudes of the parties toward each other and the effectiveness with which each can pursue its distinct agenda, and that therefore it also affects the ability of the parties to develop and sustain participative programs" (Wever 1989, 601).

Cooke and Meyer (1990) agreed with Wever as they sought to explain corporate labor relations strategies in terms of structural factors. By this these researchers meant the collective bargaining structure of the company—the number of its facilities that were unionized. And this, in turn, meant the operational and financial structure of the company—labor costs, the number of its plants, average plant size, and the ratio of costs of goods to sales.

Studies of organizational effectiveness demonstrate the systems orientation of applied research in organizational behavior and industrial relations. Hamer and Wazeter compared a goal-centered model of organizational effectiveness with a natural systems perspective: "In a natural systems perspective, the organization's overarching goal is to maintain its existence and viability without depleting its internal and external resources. Here the question of effectiveness is a much broader one: namely, how well the organization has acquired and used its resources in an environment that keeps changing" (Hamer and Wazeter 1993). Durkeim's influence is again evident as the authors of this study and others like it stressed the integrative functions of the system, when viewed as a social system. Hamer and Wazeter found that a union mentality or a "perception of the union as a political interest group representing [members] rather than merely . . . an association that meets and confers" was one of the most important factors in guaranteeing the union's continued existence and therefore its effectiveness (Hamer and Wazeter 1993, 314). The systems view advanced by Weber and Durkheim in the late 1950s continues to be an important influence on today's research in organizational behavior.

The Influence of Marx, Weber, and Durkheim
on Current Views of the Employment Relationship

Seen together, Durkheim, Weber, and Marx describe a full spectrum of possibilities for societal relationships—ranging from harmony (a society with a high degree of functional coherence and integration) to revolution. Sociologists disagree on the relative emphasis to be given to either end of the spectrum when studying a typical social system. In industrial relations, likewise, scholars disagree about the degree of emphasis to be given to social harmony, resolvable class conflict, or revolution as characteristics of work societies.

At one extreme are the British utopian socialists of the early nineteenth century, perhaps best represented by Robert Owen (1771–1858). His model communal village established in southwest Indiana was named New Harmony (founded in 1825). Patterned after his famous New Lanark community in Britain, the Midwestern experiment was designed to increase productivity and profit through dramatic improvements in the working conditions of employees. Though New Harmony was not a success, Owen went on to help found an early British labor union and ultimately was responsible for establishing the international cooperative movement launched in Rochdale, England, in 1844. Owen's belief in harmonious relationships is reflected today in the call for greater worker-management cooperation in all types of business enterprises.

At the other extreme are industrial relations scholars who emphasize the irreconcilable contradictions of industrial society. Richard Hyman, for example, wrote that "only a total transformation of the whole structure of control . . . can resolve the current contradictions within the organization of work and in social and economic life more generally" (Hyman 1975, 203). Rather than ask why workers were not motivated to work harder than they did, Burawoy (1979) instead asked why employees in a machine shop worked as hard as they did given that their effort served to enrich those who owned the capital of the firm. He concluded that the production game—with its intricate social relationships—captured employee interest and loyalty. Individual monetary incentives arranged by the capitalist were insufficient to gain the worker's consent to cooperate in the production process.

Most present-day industrial relations scholars occupy a position somewhere between the extreme positions of the neo-Marxists and the utopian socialists. For the moment, this broad grouping of scholars will be called pluralists, but in the next chapter, better distinctions will be made among the various schools of thought encompassed by pluralism. As noted earlier, the pluralist tradition argues that industrial relations problems are best resolved through multiple sources of power in industrial enterprises (Webb and Webb 1897). The argument in chapter 1 (that actors in an industrial relations system will try to achieve mid-point positions between control that is centralized in the firm, government, labor union, or market) is a pluralist one.

Pluralism posits that unions and management can reach stable contracts through bargaining, the best of which are resolved with a minimum of outside interference and agreed to by those who experience the problems on a day-to-day basis. Like Weber, pluralists argue that the world consists of various classes or strata and that the relationships among classes is one of permanent tension rather than revolutionary conflict or social harmony. In the pluralist tradition, society's norms and values hold the system together, but stability can only be achieved by accepting the opposing roles of industrial groups who are in conflict.

Talcott Parsons

Pluralist assumptions are well embedded in the formal theories of Talcott Parsons (1902–1979), perhaps sociology's most important systems theorist. Like Durkheim, Parsons also subscribed to the functionalist school of thought: society had certain basic needs (or functions) among which were the preservation of the social order, the delivery of goods and services, and the care of children. Society was also self-regulating and self-maintaining (Parsons 1951). In an address before the American Sociological Association in 1959, Parsons suggested that a sociological ideology was emerging in the 1950s—one that would supersede the previously more individualistic perspectives of psychology and economics. The sociological perspective placed stress on conformity or "the problem of constraints on individual freedom" (Smelser 1988, 554). In the 1980s and 1990s, it is hard to argue that a sociological focus on community has superseded the individualism embedded in psychology and economics, at least not in the United States. Nevertheless, much work in the social sciences reflects a

Parsonian emphasis on the stability of social systems, the constraints on individual behavior, and the processes that dictate against revolutionary change.

The social systems perspective of Parsons and other sociologists of the functionalist school is particularly relevant for industrial relations scholars because of the evolutionary changes that have occurred in social systems over time. One of the more significant changes in European and American society has been industrialization, and with it the development of labor unions. In the American context, industrialization seems to have occurred in an evolutionary, not revolutionary way. American sociologists of the 1950s described the American and European experience as follows:

> America's postwar sociologists portrayed pre-industrial society as coherent and slowly changing. They saw industrialization as a general process with its own powerful rationale. They conceived of social stratification as a comprehensive system of ranking that spanned a whole society and cut across the worlds of work, politics, and leisure. According to those views, the logic of industrialization—with its demands for individualistic competition, mobility, and general standards of evaluation—entailed a new system of stratification. The new system contradicted, challenged, and eventually displaced the old. All this happened as part of a broader, revolutionary process of modernization. (Granovetter and Tilly 1988, 176)

Postwar sociologists traced out a process where one organization of society, whose level in the strata was based on income and prestige, was replaced by another. According to this view, classes did not control the process of economic development; rather, the logic of industrialism produced a new stratification of the social system. The logic of industrialism has played an important role in industrial relations theory as well (see Barbash 1984), and, as will be shown in the next chapter, systems theory has led industrial relations scholars to emphasize the norms and values of three main actors in the industrial relations system—labor, management, and government (Dunlop 1958). Yet the evolutionary view of many sociologists and industrial relations scholars may overlook two factors glossed over in systems theory: in Granovetter and Tilly's words, struggle and division.

The Attack on Systems Theory: Conflict and Struggle

Does a stable industrial relations system exist over long periods of time? Does a social system of any sort exist? Is it helpful to create such a construct of the mind—identifying actors, their norms, and their values? A major stream of thought within sociology argues that systems theory is not helpful. These arguments take several different forms:

In 1961 Dennis Wrong warned against "an oversocialized" view of human nature, chastised systems theorists for propounding this view, and put forth an alternative psychological view, using psychoanalytic and other perspectives. That is also the thrust of the several phenomenological perspectives, the major focuses of which are on individual and interactive monitoring of meanings; they tend to regard society as constructed of and sustained by these activities. Utilizing an entirely different kind of psychology—social behaviorism—as his vehicle, George Homans nevertheless agreed with these critics that the individual in his or her matrix of social rewards is the fundamental unit of analysis, and that social regularities and institutional behavior are in effect derivable from individual actions. (Smelser 1988, 11 citing Wrong 1961, Blumer 1969, Garfinkel 1967)

Because of their systems view, pluralists within the field of industrial relations could argue that management would accept and negotiate with the labor movement which in turn would be supported by government. From this perspective, the management of a particular firm would not be likely to set its own strategic policy that included union avoidance. If, however, the systems view is flawed—as Wrong, Blumer, Garfinkle, and Homans contended—industrial relations scholars cannot simply assume that management will accept and negotiate with labor unions. Instead, the strategies, motivations, and idiosyncrasies of firms, individual managers, and individual employees must be explained.

One can readily see why the sociological debate over systems theory has been so heated. If Homans is correct, the legitimacy of sociology as a field of study separate from psychology or economics is brought severely into question. In addition, the activity of institutions (labor unions, business firms) would not need to be studied independently of the actions of their members. These activities would be derivable from the actions, needs, and desires of the individuals who built them—the strategies that individuals themselves had chosen. (As a good example, see the study by Jurgens et al. [1993] of the transformation of East German industrial relations).

Homans' challenge to systems theory is serious and far-reaching enough, but a second challenge to social systems theory, derived from the natural sciences, has even more far-reaching implications—in effect, questioning the legitimacy of all of the social sciences. The biologist, E. O. Wilson (1975), argued that most individual human behavior was biologically, not socially, determined. Wilson claimed that genetics should thus be considered the main source of individual behavior, not society. If there are tensions and conflict at work, it is because aggressive behavior has been preprogrammed in individuals through the long evolution of the species.

In industrial relations, Wilson's view was at least partly reflected by Wheeler when he argued that to some degree industrial conflict is rooted in the stable biological characteristics of individuals—their inherent tendencies toward aggression (Wheeler 1985). Strike behavior, conflict in the workplace, and other problems of the employment relationship should be contained and tolerated through law and organizational policy. But there is less need to understand the labor problem as a function of society's structure. Furthermore, policies directed at reducing conflict may not work because of the biological nature of conflict. Wilson's approach, when taken at its extreme, challenges the core assumptions of all of the social sciences, arguing that the biological system is more important for predicting human behavior than anything that might be called a social system. Coupled with Homans' thinking, all behavior then becomes a matter of understanding one's biological makeup and origins.

The above schools of thought would dispense with systems theory altogether or, as in the case of Wilson, shift emphasis from social to biological systems. Other sociological thinking, both past and present, challenges systems theory without abandoning it completely, and it is here that most industrial relations scholars would position themselves. The divisions within society are well recognized, and it is assumed that both conflict and struggle will occur because of those divisions. But more radical predictions about the systemic outcome of conflict (revolution) are replaced by an emphasis on the ongoing and shifting bases for conflict among various groups within society. Social science theory is accepted as valid and systems theory, though viewed as flawed, is accepted at least in part.

By focusing on conflict, a number of sociologists have objected to one important aspect of systems theory, at least when described by functionalists—namely, the emphasis on equilibrium and stability. Turner labels theories of conflict, which do not emphasize equilibrium and stability, as dialectical theories (Turner 1982, 181). In such theories, an inequality in the distribution of resources (land, income, or power) causes conflict, which in turn causes a reorganization of the social system. In dialectical theories, the reorganization of the system itself reveals again a new inequality in resource distribution that sets off a new cycle of conflict. A dialectical theory, "concentrate[s] on more severe and violent conflicts" (Turner 1982, 181). Functional theories of conflict, on the other hand "focus on less severe and violent conflicts and on their consequences for promoting integration with and between conflict parties and for increasing over-all system adaptability and flexibility" (Turner 1982, 181).

Industrial relations scholars rely on both dialectical and functional theories of conflict to explain behavior in industrial settings. Pluralists, for example, want to know how to balance power in society so that conflict can be resolved through bargaining. If power is balanced sufficiently (a pluralism of power is achieved), then conflict and bargaining can help to integrate the interests of labor and management. Conflict enables the industrial relations system to become adaptable and flexible to changes in economic conditions. Functional theories of conflict are useful for identifying the sources of conflict and for describing the integrating effects of conflict on the system as a whole.

Other industrial relations scholars argue that pluralists focus on narrow and trivial kinds of conflict (Fox 1973; Kochan et al. 1986). Functional theories of conflict cannot explain what occurs when periodic spells of severe or violent conflict lead to a significant transformation of the entire social system. What are the preconditions for such conflict? What explains the behavior of individuals when the constraints of the old social system are removed?

The preconditions and the effects of transformational conflict have been addressed by several sociologists—radical and not so radical. Marxist preconditions for violent conflict are the following: a concentration of capital in the hands of a few powerful industrialists, a resulting instability of the economic system with periodic spells of boom and bust, a falling rate of profit, and a rising level of unemployment induced by mechanization. But other explanations for workplace conflict have been proposed by sociologists who do not necessarily subscribe to Marx's radical view of history. Two good examples are Ralf Dahrendorf (1959) and Lewis Coser (1956).

For Dahrendorf, social conflict emerged because of inequality in authority. Dahrendorf assumed that a social order is maintained through institutions in which power and authority result in the assignment of two main roles for the members of organizations: a role for those who rule and a role for those who are ruled. Rulers want to use their authority to maintain the status quo. Those who are ruled want to redistribute power and authority. During some periods of time, the acceptance of authority relationships within organizations is a powerful force for social stability. During other periods of time, however, people become aware of their different interests, engage in conflict, and eventually redistribute authority, thereby creating a new group of individuals who rule and who are ruled (Turner 1982, 141).

The potential for social conflict could be increasing in the world economy of today as new "rulers" emerge. World markets now complement and sometimes supplant national and local markets. Vast changes in communications create the opportunity for a whole new structure of authority to occur within worldwide business firms and alliances. New elites with worldwide experience and technical skills in financial and organizational management are in demand and are being placed in positions of authority both in business and in government. If Dahrendorf is right, these new elites will want to maintain the status quo, while others will eventually challenge their authority, setting the stage for new social conflict.

Though Dahrendorf was quite clear about the way conflict occurs, he was less clear in specifying the conditions under which "various patterns of organization [are] likely to be created, maintained, and changed" (Turner 1982, 151). Coser, on the other hand, spelled out quite specifically the conditions under which conflict emerged. Unlike Dahrendorf, Coser emphasized the effect that conflict had on the parties who were engaged in it and on society as a whole. "People's involvement in and commitment to pursue . . . conflict . . . increas[es] the demarcation of boundaries, centralization of authority, ideological solidarity, and suppression of dissent and deviance within each of the conflict parties" (Turner 1982, 169). In other words, in a new, international economy one should expect to find institutions that emphasize an "us versus them" attitude—institutions that will ask individuals to decide "are you with us or against us?" These institutions may also be quite ideological. Communism as an ideology has suffered tremendous setbacks, but if Coser is right, another ideology may simply take its place with similar centralization of authority and suppression of dissent. For proponents of democracy, these are not welcome predictions. Coser's thinking, though, involves other more positive outcomes as well.

According to Coser, conflict ultimately increases the adaptability of the entire social system toward change. As a consequence, Coser differs significantly from Dahrendorf—Coser stressing how frequent, low-intensity conflict leads social systems to change gradually over time. Nevertheless, by examining Coser's preconditions for the emergence of particularly strong or violent conflict, Dahrendorf's more radical transformations of power can also be understood.

Coser argued that conflict is likely to be more violent if it is over issues that are not realistic. By realistic issues, Coser meant those that involved "the pursuit of specific aims against real sources of hostility, with some estimation of the costs to be incurred in such pursuit" (Turner 1982, 163). Likewise, the more rigid the system in which the conflict occurs and the more the conflict concerns core values, the more violent the conflict. If the above conditions are strongly present, individuals who have been deprived of authority in a social system will be more likely to withdraw their sense of legitimacy in the system and to engage in conflict. Today's particularly intense conflicts between U.S. labor and management over use of replacement workers revolve around such core values and thus could be expected to provoke violence. Any new legislation that deals with this conflict will undoubtedly be hard fought and could result in a significant transformation of the U.S. industrial relations system.

Dahrendorf and Coser together have developed a theory of conflict that can apply to practically all relationships in society. For students of industrial relations, the differentiation between conflict that leads to a reorganization of the social system and conflict that leads to further societal integration is crucial. Some may believe that wholesale changes in authority over multinational firms and the breakdown of the ability of separate countries to control their own economies are now forcing conflict away from its potentially integrating role and toward one that promises a full-scale reorganization of the worldwide social and economic system. Others might point to different forces (new technologies in communication and transportation, internationalization of markets) that could help to integrate production processes and, with them, social and economic systems.

Bargaining Over Societal Relationships:
A Modern-day Synthesis

Many of today's sociologists are working to create a compromise between social systems theorists and their detractors. Ironically, they owe much to the scholar who first set in motion the reactions and counterreactions described above—Karl Marx, himself. Granovetter and Tilly describe the modern Marxist influence as follows:

A new scholarly generation . . . [of sociologists is] more sympathetic to Marxist statements of problems (if not necessarily to conventional Marxist answers), more skeptical of the autonomous impact of technology, less convinced that "societies" are meaningful actors, more sensitive to the exercise of power and the influence of national states, more inclined to think in terms of class than of stratification, more concerned to root their analyses in history. Conflict figures much more prominently in their accounts of industrial change. (Granovetter and Tilly 1988, 176)

The overall approach of Granovetter and Tilly is, in fact, a good example of how ideas can be combined both from systems theorists and their critics—and it is highly relevant for industrial relations. In true systems style, Granovetter and Tilly have constructed a social system comprised of five actors: capitalists, workers, households, governments, and organizations (organizations include employers' organizations, unions, professional associations, and political parties). Yet these authors did not emphasize the system per se. Rather, they focused on two main processes: (1) the process of ranking jobs according to status or pay received, and (2) the process of sorting people into different employment categories (employed or unemployed), jobs, and firms.

The two main processes of ranking and sorting are neither self-maintaining nor automatic. In other words, the system is not functionalist as expressed by Weber, Durkheim, Parsons, or today's neoclassical labor economists. Granovetter and Tilly have argued that "little of the variation in rewards" in society could be attributed to individual performance in jobs (Granovetter and Tilly 1988, 181). Even if one strongly believes that rewards should be closely linked to performance, the real world does not yield much evidence that the link is there. Granovetter and Tilly saw little evidence of the effects of a well-functioning, competitive labor market or a good system of firm-level performance appraisal that sorts people into jobs based on each individual's productivity, at least not in the "North American and European experience over the last two centuries" (Granovetter and Tilly 1988, 177). They also saw little evidence that discrimination based on personal characteristics was mainly responsible for variation in rewards.

If one agrees with Granovetter and Tilly's depiction of the real world of social and economic systems, then there are two choices: the creation of a theory that is ideological and based on what one thinks should be the case or the creation of a theory that explains what is the reality. Granovetter and Tilly opted for the latter. These authors argued that only one real explanation remains for the variation in rewards that are a result of the United States' social and economic system: differences in rewards occur because of differences in bargaining power among the actors of the system.

Actors in a social system have different bargaining power because of the resources each brings to bargaining and because of their location in a complex web of interpersonal networks in society: "Workers' success in strikes depends, for example, not only on their ability to hold out without wages, but also on their capacity to keep out strikebreakers and to enlist the support of third parties, including government officials. And workers' ability to control employment depends on their ability to intervene in the networks employers use to search for new labor" (Granovetter and Tilly 1988, 181).

The social system created by Granovetter and Tilly does not look toward any known future point. Neither is their system presumed to be resting in some state of natural equilibrium. Rather, bargaining carries the system through time. Granovetter and Tilly focus attention on the processes within the system, not the system itself. History is, however, quite important since "inequality at a given point in time depends on the previous history of bargaining" (1988, 181).

By focusing attention on bargaining processes, Granovetter and Tilly have turned their attention to power. The notion that power depends on resources is simple common sense and does not help greatly in formulating a theory of human behavior. A theory must determine what resources can be brought together and how they might be used. One of the first and foremost resources is the ability to act as a group. Workers may act as a group vis-à-vis an employer, and employers may act as a group relative to the interests of workers as consumers. Conflict of interest among the groups is presumed with each group gathering together in defense of its own interests. In a market economy, the strength of the group depends at least in part on their ability to influence prices, and here, the economic laws of demand affect the bargaining power of workers and their protective organizations in an elastic fashion: "where the demand for a firm's products is price inelastic, the kind of labor in question [is] invulnerable to substitution, the other factors of production that might be substituted [are] in short supply, and labor costs [are] a relatively small part of the total cost of production, workers' bargaining strength increases" (Granovetter and Tilly 1988, 201). Other resources that affect a work group's bargaining power are the unity of interests of members of the group, the support of others outside the group, and the group's ability to inflict damage on the firm—either through discontinuing work effort or sabotage.

Employers, too, have resources at their disposal for bargaining. In many ways, their resources are similar to those of workers, but in one respect they differ in their control over the production process. In North America and in Western Europe, employers have typically exercised more control over production processes than workers. To be sure, workers control the degree of effort they bring to the production process, but employers control the organization of work itself. Work can be controlled through surveillance, through systems where the results of work effort are rewarded (payment by results and other types of incentive systems), and through appeals to worker loyalty (Granovetter and Tilly 1988, 202). The control system that is chosen reveals the degree of bargaining power the employer holds relative to its employees. The choice of control system and its day-to-day operation are also subjects of bargaining among actors in the broader social system.

Bargaining Theory and the Traditional Shop-floor Concerns of Industrial Sociologists

Granovetter and Tilly's framework allowed one to step through the social systems view of the world and emerge again at the shop floor. It is, after all, at the shop floor where many industrial sociologists have focused their attention in the past. Burawoy's study of a machine tool plant is a good example of the types of questions that have traditionally been of interest to the industrial sociologist (Burawoy 1979). When Burawoy selected a plant in which he could work for several months, he unwittingly selected the same one analyzed several decades earlier by Donald Roy (Roy 1952). Roy's concerns were typical of industrial sociology at the time. In this earlier study, Roy examined the establishment of group norms for the rate of production and the social constraints built into the work environment which prevented rate busting (exceeding significantly the piece rate considered normal by members of the work group.) He asked why machinists did not work harder than they did. His answer followed closely in the tradition outlined by Parsons and other systems theorists—namely that the social organization of work constrained the range of effort deemed acceptable by the group, in spite of management's interest in achieving greater work effort.

Burawoy's later approach reflected the changes in thinking of many industrial sociologists. Burawoy was impressed not by how little work was done by the machinists, but by how much. Neo-Marxist in his approach, he saw an irreconcilable conflict of interest built into the production process of the machine tool firm. Management of the firm would try to exploit its workforce in the interests of profit. As a consequence, Burawoy's main research question was just the opposite of Roy's. Burawoy asked why machine tool operators worked as hard as they did, given that their efforts would inevitably be exploited by management. His answer was noted above—that the social relations of production captured worker interest and loyalty, thereby co-opting the worker to pursue the aims of management.

Between Roy and Burawoy, one can find the full array of concerns of industrial sociologists regarding the labor problem. Some sociologists place emphasis on social control as the process that is predominant as workers and management try to resolve the labor problem. Other sociologists place primary emphasis on conflict and struggle. Still others emphasize the process of bargaining. No matter what perspective is taken, much is still to be learned. Granovetter and Tilly observed that:

> We know surprisingly little about the causal relations among labor processes, organized inequality, and the routine operations of employing organizations. Thus our arguments do not add up to a comprehensive theory of the relations between inequality and labor processes. They do, however, point toward an account in which struggles among parties having unequal resources and conflicting interests strongly affect those relations. In that respect, at least, they follow the trend of recent work in political economy. (Granovetter and Tilly 1988, 187)

Indirectly, the authors argued that no single social science discipline was sufficient to provide a comprehensive theory of inequality and labor processes. Industrial relations scholars make the same argument regarding a comprehensive theory of labor relations. In the end, Granovetter and Tilly shifted attention from sociology to political economy. Perhaps this should be of no surprise given the importance they attributed to power, conflict, and systems of control. I likewise now turn to an examination of the political economy and its potential impact on labor relations. The discussion will be familiar: systems theory; theories based on individual motivation and behavior; conflict and its resolution; control over individual behavior by those in authority; the sources, use, and abuse of power; and finally, bargaining and negotiation.

Political Science and Industrial Relations

For political science to be relevant to industrial relations, it must be related to labor problems as seen from the shop floor. As seen in the discussion above, shop-floor problems are also related to the broader social system in which work occurs. Political science could be of considerable help to industrial relations scholars and practitioners if its theories could aid in the understanding of authority, influence, control, and negotiation within organizations.

A widely accepted notion among today's political scientists is that political activity is part of a process for resolving conflicts in values through some system of authority (see, for example, Easton 1965). In the organizing framework of this book, allocation has been viewed as one of the four key activities occurring in all work settings, but to this point, allocation has been assumed to be economic. Waldo argued, however, that political activity was also a form of allocation. Instead of thinking only about how jobs or income are allocated, one should also consider how values are allocated: "All societies, even the so-called stateless ones, may be said to have a political technology. That is, they have a set of institutional arrangements for making authoritative allocations of values for society" (Waldo 1976, 18).

The work society within a business firm makes authoritative allocations of values. The best evidence for this can be seen in the firm's policy handbook. In the handbook, the firm codifies its values and the values that it must comply with legally. Anyone who has tried to put together such a handbook, will attest to the politics that surround its development. The handbook may simply put in writing what has been past practice, but the political process of defending past practice and resolving inconsistent policies from one part of the firm to another can be anything but simple. Added to the complications of the firm's internal politics are the politics of the broader society in which the firm operates. A firm may devote both time and resources to lobbying so that some policies do not have to appear in the policy handbook. To understand how policy handbooks come into being and how conflicts in values are resolved, the political scientist directs one to the political technology of society and the firm. But to understand what is meant by the term *political technology* one must first understand what the political scientist means by the state.

The political state today is considered an integral part of industrial society, but the mere idea of a political state has had a long history of development. Two writers are often referred to when tracing the idea of a political state back to its origin. Machiavelli (1469–1527) is the first to be credited with using the term *the state,* or *"lo stato,"* in his classic book *The Prince.* Somewhat later, Hobbes (1588–1629) was to use the idea of the state in an analytical sense by examining the power of the ruler in the political state. His analysis is contained in yet another classic book, *Leviathan.* The modern-day study of political science takes these classic concepts of political power and the state to examine the formal structure of political organizations and the political behavior of individual citizens.

Three broad perspectives characterize the study of political science today. First is the historical perspective. How are political states created? What happens to political states over time? Under what conditions will quite different political systems converge, come into conflict, or self-destruct? The answers to such questions can be found through analysis of governments over long periods of time; thus, it is no surprise that political science originated as a field in close association with history.

Within the historical perspective, a writer of considerable importance is, again, Marx. In his historical approach to change in the capitalist system, Marx also spoke to change in the political system. But Marx's ideas were more antipolitical than political. He predicted the declining importance of the state (its withering away) as the economic system changed from capitalism to socialism and then to communism. For this reason, perhaps, his influence has not been as strong on political scientists as on sociologists. Nevertheless, for both sociologists and political scientists, Marxist conceptions of class structure have had a strong impact.

A second important perspective is to view the political system within its broader societal context. In American universities, political science was originally associated with history. In the period before World War I, "political scientists argued that the crucial relationship of political science is with sociology, conceived as the study of the social realm entire" (Waldo 1976, 75). The development of the idea of a state, in fact, closely parallels the development of systems theory in sociology since a political state, virtually by definition, is a social system. Any government is a formal organization but the question that has confronted political science as well as sociology is whether the state is best analyzed as a system or as the sum of all the behaviors of individuals who are citizens of the state.

In answering the question of whether the state or the individual should be the focus of analysis, political scientists reply: either. Political science can be defined as the study of individual political behavior, authority relationships over individuals, and the use of power by individuals to attain political objectives. It can also be defined as the study of authoritarianism and democracy, socialism and corporatism. Political science today is defined to include all of the above and more.

Systems Theory and Political Science

Taking a systems perspective on the field, Waldo argued that: "the main and characteristic political thought of the modern period divides itself into three categories: that concerned with creating and justifying the modern state, that directed toward changing and improving the state, and that seeking to destroy or transcend the state" (Waldo 1976, 12). The various schools of sociological thought discussed earlier can be incorporated into political thought by using the same three-part classification. Systems theorists who focus on social control and the maintenance of social systems develop theory to justify the modern state—in particular, the American political system with its various checks and balances. Conflict theorists, on the other hand, have much to say about the modern state as it changes and is improved over time. Finally, radical theories focus on predicting the set of conditions that would lead citizens to destroy and transcend the state.

The systems view of political science as described by Waldo facilitates an understanding of broad political movements and their relationships with labor unions. In the United States, for example, the labor movement has usually helped to maintain the social and political system by negotiating within its accepted limits. In Europe, on the other hand, labor movements and socialist political parties have often formed alliances that are in conflict with the political status quo (see Sturmthal 1972). And in Eastern Europe (Poland in particular) labor unions have indeed destroyed and transcended the old political state. In the systems view of politics, the state, employer's associations, and the labor movement all affect the industrial relations system, but making predictions about the outcome depends on an understanding of power and negotiation.

Labor and the Politics of Influence

A good example of the difficulty in making predictions about how an industrial relations system may be transformed is the debate among historians and political scientists over the reason for passage of the U.S. National Labor Relations Act (NLRA) and Social Security Act in 1935. For some, the NLRA benefited capitalists by preventing a wholesale breakdown of the social system. Thus the NLRA should be considered conservative in outlook, and it should come as no surprise that subsequent legislation would weaken U.S. labor and lead to the current decline in the percent of the labor force unionized. For others, the state had considerable autonomy from any influence group, whether capitalist or labor. From this view, New Deal legislation was a pragmatic response to the unique conditions of the Great Depression. Still others have hypothesized that capitalists responded to the unorganized and spontaneous disruptions of individual workers and pressured the state to reform the system. Finally are those who view the changes of the New Deal as a response to the labor movement and to the increased influence of radical political organizations (for a discussion of all these views, see Goldfield 1989).

More importantly, perhaps, is the fact that each of the above views could result in a different prediction about the transformation of the industrial relations system that may be occurring now. Will the new global economy carry the stamp of labor movements and radical political groups the world over? Will any and all reforms simply reflect the interests of worldwide capital investors? Answers to these questions would help one to understand the politics of the North American Free Trade Agreement (NAFTA), but unfortunately scholars have not yet reached agreement on the forces affecting the last significant transformation of the American industrial relations system, let alone the present one.

Labor and the Corporatist State

In the examples above, the influence of labor's representatives on politics was indirect—through the lobbying done by labor federations or through other allied social movements. In a second interesting case, the labor movement becomes an independent actor in a country's political system. It does not act merely as a lobbying group or as a political party, but as an independent, national representative of employee interests in the economic system. Under such circumstances, the labor movement and the state can, together, create a national system of authority that makes the authority shared between management and labor at the shop floor more complex. If the state, itself, assumes authority over the economic system and co-opts both labor and management, the result may become what political scientists have called a corporatist state.

The concept of corporatism has considerable importance for industrial relations, but it is one that has generated its share of controversy within political science. To understand what corporatism is, one must also understand what corporatism is not. Corporatism describes a particular kind of relationship between the state and various groups of citizens who share common economic interests; but it is not pluralism. Earlier in this chapter, pluralists were described as persons who believe that workplace conflicts can best be resolved by creating multiple sources of power within society. For pluralists, negotiation among groups is expected to result in the peaceful resolution of conflict. In the more general political context, pluralism can be defined as a system in which interest groups: "are organized into an unspecified number of multiple, voluntary, competitive, non hierarchically ordered and self-determined . . . categories which are not specially licensed, recognized, subsidized, created or otherwise controlled . . . by the state" (Schmitter 1979, 15).

In a pluralist industrial relations system, the state does not subsidize union organizations and does not enact complex legislation governing the activities of unions, once organized. The British industrial relations system is often cited as an example of a pluralist system. British law supports a union's right to organize and to strike, but until more recent years, it regulated union activities very little.

A corporatist system, on the other hand, is one in which there is: "(1) state *structuring* of groups that produces a system of officially sanctioned, non-competitive, compulsory interest associations; (2) state *subsidy* of these groups; and (3) state-imposed *constraints* on demand-making, leadership, and internal governance" (Collier and Collier 1979, 968). In labor relations, a corporatist state may encourage the formation of a single labor federation, appoint some of its leaders, help to finance its operations, and in other more subtle ways make it beholden to government. Labor legislation both induces labor to become a partner with government in the economic system and constrains labor's actions once engaged. Political scientists typically point to various Latin American countries as examples of corporatist arrangements—for example, Argentina under Peron (1946–1955) and Brazil under Vargas (1930–1945).

The hierarchical nature of the arrangements of corporatism are important. A government that operates under a system of corporatism will try to structure the various organizations representing labor or management into a hierarchy of authority. Given a hierarchy of authority, government can control all the members of a few carefully constructed interest groups while they, in turn, try to control government. The result is a mutual dependence between labor and government and an implicit narrowing of labor's choices for resolving shop-floor problems. In a corporatist state, a militant rank-and-file response to unsafe working conditions could be defused by labor leaders if the government's objective were for rapid economic growth, despite the high human cost. Government replaces management as the main source of authority within the economic system—laying claim to its authority by arguing that it alone has sufficient information and expertise to plan the long-range economic development strategy for the nation.

In a global economy, an understanding of corporatism has become quite important for students of industrial relations and human resource management. International trade does not always occur according to the rules of comparative advantage. In a world of managed trade, nations may guide economic development by subtle and not so subtle coercion of both labor and management. If corporatism underlies trading patterns, is some rule of fairness desirable to "level the playing field" for trade? If so, one reenters the world of rules that are reasonable as originally outlined by Commons.

In a country's own domestic economy, an understanding of corporatism may also be important because of the potential impact that corporatism and centralized bargaining can have on the economic performance of the country as a whole. Corporatist countries may pursue, in addition to their policies governing trade, policies of wage restraint which seek to achieve a rapid rate of economic growth with low unemployment and low inflation. This objective may be achieved by a national agreement among labor, management, and government regarding a reasonable rate of wage increase.

Corporatism is a matter of degree and it may not be a stable political form over the long term. At one extreme is a government that excludes labor or management representatives from any influence on the overall direction of the economic system. At the other extreme is a government that guarantees labor the right to organize and then does not interfere as representatives of labor and management bargain with each other. In between these two extremes, corporatism takes a variety of forms. In some, government plays a leading role in directing the actions of the other partners (state corporatism). In others, the actions of government are quite indirect, with strong and independent roles being played by labor and management (societal corporatism) (Collier and Collier 1979, 979). In either form, corporatism may not exist long term. The co-optation of other actors by government may eventually lead to disillusionment as labor and corporate members come to feel that neither labor unions nor employers' associations are acting as their agents under corporatism. The model on which this book is based predicts that employers and union members alike will then turn to the market, asking it, in effect, to serve as agent for their interests. As employers and employees abandon their respective representative organizations for the market, corporatism breaks down. This may help to explain why, even in Sweden, centralized negotiations between labor and management at the national level have recently begun to break down. (See Wallerstein 1990 for additional thoughts on explaining the shifts between centralized and decentralized bargaining.)

Authority Relationships and Politics in Individual Firms

Government is what students of sociology would call a formal organization and often plays a key role in the industrial relations system. But formal organizations, under the right circumstances, can also be viewed as governments. To analyze a business firm as if it were a government, attention must be turned from the systems view of political science to one based more on individual attitudes and behavior. Waldo again has provided direction by defining political science in terms of various types of individual behavior. He argued that political science can be defined as an analysis of "state authority versus private rights, [an] interest in domestic affairs versus [an] interest in relations among states, [or an] orientation toward past versus [an] orientation toward future, regime preference" (Waldo 1976, 12). The first of these three potential definitions, the analysis of authority relationships versus private rights, is critical for understanding certain types of plant-level industrial relations problems. It is a theme that has concerned a relatively small number of political scientists whose work has often combined theory from sociology and political science in a manner quite relevant for industrial relations.

Authority at the shop floor depends primarily on deciding who controls the production process. No matter how authoritarian the system, management does not have absolute control since, ultimately, each employee retains control over the degree of work effort that will be expended. Management must entice, cajole, threaten, or otherwise persuade its own employees to work. The process of eliciting work effort is both social and political.

Eliciting work effort is social because of the shop-floor norms that control the pace of work. It is political (1) because of the rights that may or may not be guaranteed the worker and (2) because of the question of authority—is the authority of management accepted by the workforce (is it legitimate)?

Employee Rights and the Employment Contract

Basic industrial rights are guaranteed through the political system, but in the market economies of western nations, these rights are sometimes so taken for granted that it is easy to forget the role played by politics—both in establishing and in maintaining industrial rights. From an individual's perspective, undoubtedly the most important industrial right is in the form of a guarantee that only labor services will be bought and sold in the market—a person is not to be bought and sold like a commodity. Freedom from slavery is guaranteed through the implicit or explicit employment contract. The employment contract specifies the obligations of an employer in terms of expected wages and working conditions, but it does not, in a free-market economy, oblige an employee to stay with a firm for any given length of time. Employees are free to terminate the employment relationship at any time. Employers, on the other hand, are often permitted to end the relationship only if the quality of labor services provided by an employee is judged deficient according to a set of clear criteria. In other words, an employer's right to fire an employee at will may be limited by law or by the employment contract.

The political system guarantees an employee's right to terminate an employment contract at any time, but how absolute is that right in practice? The right is only absolute if the state also guarantees income to citizens who quit their jobs voluntarily. In traditional society, this form of guarantee fell to the clan or the tribe, but in the less personal, modern industrialized societies an income guarantee is rarely provided unless the termination is due to layoff or discharge. The practical importance of the right to terminate employment contracts voluntarily is thus quite limited:

> It is easy to overlook the coordinating functions of market systems, so much do we take them for granted. . . . Coordination is only achieved at a price, however. A hypothetical pure unmodified market system would be extraordinary—and intolerable—in that it would strip the individual of all but one claim on other members of the society. He could not ask for their help in distress as he can in traditional premarket systems in which he is an accepted member of the tribe or clan and deserves their compassion. In a pure market system his claim on others would be established if and only if he had something to offer in exchange. . . .
>
> How much I can accomplish and how effectively I can protect myself through exchange depends in large part on what I own and can offer in exchange . . . if we are all born into a world in which property rights are already assigned, as indeed they are, [it does not] follow that exchange supports our freedom unless we own a great deal. (Lindblom 1977, 39, 45)

A logical extension of the industrial right to withdraw labor services individually from the firm is the right to withdraw labor services collectively (or the right to strike). The right to collective bargaining may mean that the right to withdraw services collectively has also been guaranteed, thereby forcing employers to bargain. Like the right to terminate employment contracts, the right to strike depends on the practical ability of employees to sustain themselves during periods when they are not at work. Thus the right to accumulate strike funds, the right to qualify for food stamps (in the United States), the right to unemployment compensation, and the government's guarantee to sustain full employment are all political issues that indirectly affect the right to bargain collectively.[1]

Private Property, Employer Rights, and Authority

Of equal, if not greater, importance than individual or collective contract rights are the rights of employers in systems based on the principle of private property. Employers, because of their property rights, may wield authority if the state defends their right to use property as they wish. But will the authority be considered legitimate by the firm's employees? The answer is crucial since employers with legitimate authority may choose among a wide variety of control systems to coordinate production—some of which involve the participation of employees and some of which do not. Employers whose authority is not perceived to be legitimate will have to rely on force or coercion to coordinate production which may exacerbate labor problems.

Authority is legitimate if one member of an organization is willing to accept the orders of another and sanction them with his/her approval. A person may sometimes accept authority because of hereditary rights. A sovereign's authority is accepted because of birth. In industrial relations, customary procedure may be the basis for authority. If it has always been done this way before, and if no one wishes to challenge past practice, then future actions will simply be based on the past.

Rights may also be based on property. I may accept the authority of the owners of small businesses to arrange production in whatever strange and wonderful way they wish since the benefit or loss falls largely to them. But why should I accept the authority of management in a large business enterprise? Management does not have hereditary rights to authority and does not own the firm. In the absence of hereditary and property rights, how then does managerial authority become legitimate?

Dahl (1970) argued that by examining the desired choices of subordinates and comparing them with the choices made by superiors, one could understand the boundaries for legitimate authority. In the simplest of all cases, authority is legitimate if the choices made by a person in authority are the same as those that I would make. How likely is this to occur? Not very, according to Dahl: "If I wish to live among others, as I most emphatically do, then either we must all spontaneously agree all the time or we must have some way of dealing with our disagreements. The whole history of mankind, as I read it argues against the possibility of perfect harmony" (Dahl, 9).

If my desired choices are not the same as the person in authority, I can try to dominate the organization by naked force. But others will not accept my authority willingly since they also are following the same simple principle—accept authority only if your choices are the same as the choices of the one who is in authority. By definition, however, my choices are not the same as others. The domination strategy is therefore doomed to fail.

I can try to have my authority accepted through use of what Dahl called "the royal lie." I can argue that my preferences are really those of everyone else, despite all appearances to the contrary. Or I can argue that I have been divinely appointed and, therefore, my preferences carry more weight than others. Finally, I can treat other points of view as equally legitimate to mine and accept in authority someone whose views reflect those who are in the majority. Even so, there may be some values so important to me that they must be protected, regardless of the views of the majority. Under such circumstances, I would only join an organization which, from the outset, protected my basic values from being overturned by majority rule. The result is democratic, constitutional government based on majority rule. Authority based on a royal lie or on divine rights will be accepted as legitimate only temporarily in a modern, industrial society, if at all. Thus, Dahl's argument leads to a strong presumption that legitimate authority will ultimately be based on democratic, constitutional government—whether in a national government or in a private firm.

The authority of most American managers is not legitimate according to the above criteria. Some top-level managers in family-owned firms might appeal to property and hereditary rights as a basis for authority, but the vast majority of managers cannot justify their authority so easily. Even though participation in decision making may be characteristic of some firms, it is certainly not the democratic, constitutional government described by Dahl. Stockholders have limited, democratic rights, but they are not vested with the day-to-day authority over the firm's operations: "In most large corporations top management selects the board of directors. Shareholders generally make little effort to involve themselves in the day to day operations of the firm. They are, for the most part, interested in return on investment not enterprise governance" (Adams 1988b, 184).

Authority can still be legitimate even if members of the firm do not behave like the participants in a New England town meeting. The purest form of democratic rule presumes that anyone whose views reflect the majority can be accepted as a person in authority. But this presumption gives no credit to the differences in competence that may exist among members of an organization. A purely democratic form of governance would have passengers and crew members deciding together on how a plane would be flown. In such circumstances, majority rule yields to competence in that passengers are more than willing to accept the authority of the captain for piloting the plane, as long as the pilot's competence is not questioned. So, to some degree, in all business enterprises authority based on broad rights to participate in decisions yields to the competence of management—both for seeking out technical solutions to production problems and for overall coordination of the enterprise.

A second limit on democratically based authority is what Dahl referred to as economy. Democratic decisions take time, especially if everyone who is affected by a decision is permitted the time to voice an opinion. Compromises must always be made between time spent in making decisions and time spent in other productive activity. Thus authority will sometimes be granted to managers simply to protect the limited amount of time that exists for all of the activities of the firm. The larger the organization, the more constraining will be the principle of economy on governance.

Since firms vary both in size and in the specialized competence of the members of the firm who must coordinate its activities, what would be a highly illegitimate use of power in one organization might be legitimate in another.

Similarly, governance structures should vary from firm to firm and from country to country. Labor unions, works councils, quality circles, consultative decision-making bodies, and democratic election procedures for members of the board of directors or for managers themselves are all examples of the variation. Nevertheless, in the United States, as well as most industrialized free-market countries, businesses are governed mainly by management: "Even though all of the nations of the industrialized, market oriented world are governed by democratic procedures the modal form of governance in industry is weak to moderate constitutionalism. Everywhere in the West managers have been able to reserve to themselves discretion in regard to a wide range of issues which in the national sphere would be open for debate and liable to decision by representatives of the citizenry" (Adams 1988b, 183).

The establishment in the 1930s of the right to bargain collectively changed the governance form in the United States by granting labor organizations the right to joint decision making largely in the areas of wages and working conditions. Despite this change, Dahl believed that the use of power was by and large not the legitimate kind of authority to be expected from a more comprehensive governance structure. "The orthodox 'private property' view says that the firm ought to be governed by the people who own it. [But] why should people who own shares be given the privileges of citizenship in the government of the firm when citizenship is denied to other people who also make vital contributions to the firm . . . [namely] employees and customers . . . and the general public" (Dahl 1970, 122).

Two decades have passed since Dahl's harsh judgment of American business. In that time much experimentation has occurred with employee participation in business decisions. In firms with autonomous work groups, employees and their managers are assumed to have relatively equal expertise regarding day-to-day production problems. As a consequence, managers sometimes serve as consultants to the groups of employees they supervise, with employees gaining the right to propose changes in production procedures and to carry them out. The change in authority relationships is an implicit change in the governance of the firm. The change in governance, in turn, can lead to more creative and more permanent innovations in production processes. An added benefit is a rise in employee satisfaction with work.

The experiments with participation are many, but the evidence is not good regarding the degree of actual participation that exists. Adams is not convinced by arguments that additional democratic reforms are unnecessary because the degree of participation is already high:

There is a considerable amount of evidence which suggests that current institutions do not provide entirely satisfactory checks on managerial decision making. . . . The most extensive study of employee participation in the liberal democratic world concluded that employees have little influence on most managerial decisions. Even in countries like Sweden and West Germany, which are considered to have advanced employee participation schemes, employees have only a modest capacity to influence the making of enterprise policy. (Adams 1988b, 186)

A system of collective bargaining is still an effective means of participation in managerial decisions—admittedly for a limited range of topics and at irregular intervals. Nevertheless, it changes the authority structure of industrial firms. In the United States, collective bargaining can be viewed as a simple form of governance where rules are legislated across the bargaining table and are enforced through grievance procedures and arbitration.

Political science theory is therefore useful if directed at the establishment of rights and the creation of legitimate authority, both at the shop floor and within the total economic system. At the shop floor, the principles of economy and expertise have demonstrated how authority can be perceived as legitimate—even when democratic, constitutional governance has been greatly compromised. At the level of the economy, a political state can constrain the ability of labor to challenge the authority of management by inducing labor leaders to accept corporatist control.

Summary

This book begins with a framework that, on the one hand, describes a system with several potential centers of control. In that sense, my framework is firmly within the tradition of Weber, Parsons, and Dunlop. Yet it is not a static one. It presumes that individuals, in an effort to avoid being drawn too heavily toward one or another center of control, will construct for themselves institutions that act as agents for their own individual interests. Individuals must be constantly alert to the possibility, however, that an agent may ultimately pull the individual toward one of the centers of control rather than protecting against such a possibility.

An individual may turn to a large employer's internal labor market for protection from the insecurities of the external market, assuming that the firm's Department of Human Resources would serve as an honest agent in keeping the individual's best interests well in mind. Disillusionment may set in, and if so, the individual could then join with others to build a labor union that would serve as a new agent for protecting individuals from the employer's exercise of power and control. If the union, as agent, exercises indiscriminate control over an individual's employment relationship, the next shift could be toward government. And if all institutional protections fall short in serving the agency functions that individuals require, appeal can once again be made to the market. The overriding assumption is that individuals will build a complete social system that incorporates various agents to protect their individual members.

I do not agree with Homans or with Wilson that all behavior is individual and/or biological in its origin. The institutions of agency that are created by individuals form a social system in which the terms for employment are negotiated—the policies and procedures in the firm's employee handbook, the regulations over employment established by government, the terms of a collectively bargained contract, and the wages and working conditions established by employers and prospective job seekers in a competitive market. But I do agree with Homans and Wilson that one should be careful not to ignore the individual in the social system. It is *individual* disillusionment with an agent that leads to a search for new agents. Individual disillusionment leads to collective efforts to prevent the concentration of power in any one center of control for long periods of time.

Political science and sociology are both necessary for understanding negotiation over the rules for developing, allocating, using, and maintaining human resources. The political scientist focuses on conflicts in values and argues that political activity results from attempts to resolve conflicts in values through appeal to some higher authority. In many cases, authority is democratic and constitutional, but the need for expertise in the leadership of organizations may constrain democratic authority. In addition, the restricted amount of time available for democratic debate may further limit the possibilities for democratic control.

Sociologists have been quite divided in their approach to conflict of all kinds. Some, like Marx, see conflict as a requirement for the total transformation of society; others, like Durkheim, see conflict as a means for the continued integration of society. Industrial relations scholars, who once focused heavily on societal and organizational structure (bargaining structure, financial structure, and size of firm) for understanding conflict, have turned more recently to an analysis of strategic choices. In such analysis, conflict does not occur solely within the bounds of a predictable, self-regulating social system. Instead, individual idiosyncrasies, peculiar conditions in the external environment, the history of the organization, and the quality of its leadership all gain in importance. Strategic choices emerge that may create the conditions for more intense conflict than occurred in the self-regulating system. The choices made by individuals or by firms are harder to predict when systems are not assumed to maintain the status quo.

Chapter 5

NEO-INSTITUTIONALISTS, ECONOMICS, AND INDUSTRIAL RELATIONS

Throughout this book, I have assumed that individuals will not always be willing to accept the external market as sole agent for representing their employment interests. This differs considerably from the assumption made by classical and neoclassical economists. For them, competitive forces create wage rates and working conditions that are the best possible choice for individuals— given the technology and natural resources available to the firm. The classical and neoclassical economist assumes that the institutions of a competitive market system perform their agency functions well; individuals would not need protection from their own agents. In contrast, I have argued that individuals may try to protect themselves from the market through government, labor unions, or internal labor markets of large firms. To show support for my own assumptions, I describe several dissenting schools of thought within industrial relations and economics.

The Basic Assumptions of Classical Economics

Dissent comes naturally to many industrial relations scholars, but to understand the dissent, one must first have a good idea of the classical (and neoclassical) paradigm. Many would instantly associate classical economics with efficiency in allocating resources. Students of economics will recall the textbook definition of economics as the study of scarcity, and economists certainly do place emphasis on the advantages of markets in achieving economic efficiency. But as mentioned before (see chapter 2), classical economists like Adam Smith, David Ricardo, and Thomas Malthus were also interested in economic growth. It has, in fact, been argued that growth, not the ideal allocation of resources in an economic system, was the main theme of Smith's famous *Wealth of Nations:* "Adam Smith's major work, *The Wealth of Nations,* is a theoretical attack on mercantilism, showing that mercantilism's incumbent misallocation of economic surplus is harmful to economic growth and must be replaced by a policy of laissez faire. The main theme of the book is economic growth and a subsidiary theme is the efficient allocation of given resources" (Hsieh and Mangum 1986, 19).

Smith's famous image of the "invisible hand" was used in support of his arguments about economic growth. Free markets created and enforced by the legal framework of government would result in growth, but only if a certain degree of social harmony was assumed:

> A simplistic explanation of the invisible hand concept often implies a degree of social harmony that seems most unbelievable in reality. But to believe such harmony was inevitable was not what the classicists were saying. Indeed, they argued that such harmony, a very limited kind of harmony, would have to be created by a system of social control. The classicists envisioned such social control as being established through government and . . . [through] morals, religion, customs and education. (Hsieh and Mangum, 1986)[1]

An Overview of the Dissent from Classical and Neoclassical Economics

The classical paradigm of economics focused on whether an economic system could be expected to grow over time and specified the conditions that would most likely encourage growth—namely, a high degree of social harmony in the system. Dissenting industrial relations scholars argued that achieving social harmony would be no small matter and would necessitate understanding some of the problems of social control within organizations, especially when production occurred within the hierarchy of a large industrial firm.

Industrial relations dissent to traditional economic theory—briefly discussed in chapter 2—took both American and European forms. First were the American institutionalist economists who stressed the importance of contracts for achieving social harmony within the economic system—the Wisconsin School of institutional analysis. Names of theorists readily associated with it are Commons, Perlman, and Barbash.[2] Second were European pluralists who, unlike the institutionalists of the Wisconsin School, combined analysis of economic transactions with political transactions. While American scholars were emphasizing the labor union's role in giving workers a voice through grievance procedures and in providing limited participation in managerial decisions through collective bargaining, European scholars were busy defining workers' influence both in terms of collective bargaining and industrial democracy (works councils, worker representatives on managerial boards). Some of the scholars associated with the European pluralist tradition are G. D. H. Cole, Allen Flanders, Rudolf Meidner, and the Fabian Socialists (for example, Sidney and Beatrice Webb).

Third was another school of American institutionalist thought that focused its attention more broadly on the labor market and not as specifically on the contractual relationships between management and labor. Some American institutional labor economists—like Commons—examined how efficient economic growth could occur and yet provide sufficient security for the workforce through the construction of social insurance. Other institutional labor economists are Somers, Marshall, Kerr, Dunlop, Harbison, and Myers. Both Gerald Somers and Ray Marshall focused attention on the institutions through which training was provided to members of the workforce. Kerr, Dunlop, Harbison, and Myers used an institutional approach to study the changes in attitudes and individual behaviors that seemingly must occur as societies industrialize. Fourth are the neo-institutionalists—like Oliver Williamson—who brought the institutionalist tradition full circle. Neo-institutionalists are labor economists who use the neoclassical paradigm as a starting point for their own complaints with neoclassical theory—namely, that it produces anomalies in the pricing system for labor services.

Neo-institutionalists have not been terribly concerned with how an individual fares as an economy grows. Nor have they cared whether the market serves as a good agent for individuals—the assumption is that it does. For neo-institutionalists, the *firm* has an agency problem. The firm wants individuals to serve as its agents and to provide good services for its customers. In many instances, however, individual employees are far removed from the center of the firm's operations and can have considerable autonomy and decision-making power. The autonomy makes it difficult for the firm to contract efficiently with its agents to achieve success. An internal governance mechanism is required because long-term implicit contracts exist with the firm's employees and these contracts must be managed and enforced over time. Employees participate in the firm's decision making and therefore are willing to serve as the firm's agents.

The agency problem was very different for Wisconsin School institutionalists, for European pluralists, and for American institutional labor economists. For all of them, the agency problem was seen from the individual's perspective, not the firm's. The question raised was the following: how can business firms, labor unions, and government serve as trustworthy agents for the interests of individuals when competitive markets fail? A governance structure is often the answer—but it is generally more democratic than that envisioned by neo-institutionalists.

John R. Commons—Initiator of
Two American Institutionalist Traditions

Commons begins his book, *Institutional Economics,* by setting out his particular form of dissent from classical economics. First he points to the common ground: "I start, like economists, with scarcity, as universal for all economic theory" (1961, 6). He then spells out the principles on which his dissent from the classical paradigm is based:

> Cooperation does not arise from a *presupposed* harmony of interests, as the older economists believed. It arises from the necessity of *creating a new harmony* of interests—or at least order, if harmony is impossible— out of the conflict of interests among the hoped-for cooperators. It is the negotiational psychology of persuasion, coercion, or duress. . . . Hence, harmony is not a presupposition of economists—it is a consequence of collective action designed to maintain rules that shall govern the conflicts. (Commons 1961, 6, 7)

For Commons, markets could not be expected to harmonize all economic interests. Instead, negotiations (both private and public) would result in what he called reasonable value. In the private negotiations between labor and management, for example, a temporary harmony of interests or order could be codified into a set of rules that would facilitate cooperation—the labor contract or collective agreement that today routinely follows a set of labor negotiations. In the public arena, Commons believed that reasonable value could be established through the courts. In today's environment, Commons' ideas have become particularly relevant as lawyers seek to quantify the damages derived from discrimination in hiring procedures and as judges wrestle with the concept of comparable worth.

The market is the mechanism by which a price is usually established, but for Commons prices are also established in nonmarket settings. The mechanism by which reasonable value is established is the transaction. For establishing value, three different kinds of transactions could serve as alternatives to the market. The first is the managerial transaction which arose from "the relations of a legal superior to a legal inferior" (Commons 1961, 672). The setting of an internal schedule of compensation for a firm's employees exemplifies managerial transactions, and in firms that promote from within the managerial transaction can be quite independent of the market that exists outside the firm. Today, firms may establish reasonable pay rates for their employees by using a point system based on several criteria—experience, skills, education, and responsibility, for example. The attempt to achieve internal equity is exactly what Commons calls reasonable value derived from a managerial transaction.

The second kind of transaction is the rationing transaction. For firms that hire from labor markets in which excess numbers of workers are seeking employment and where wage rates do not clear the market, a rationing transaction will occur. Employees will be arranged in a queue waiting for each available new job. How the employer chooses from the queue of prospective workers may place some groups at a severe disadvantage compared with others. Lester Thurow (1972) extends Commons' line of thinking by arguing that such labor queues are everyday characteristics of modern labor markets. He argues further that employers select prospective employees from a queue based on a subjective assessment of their trainability. Thus, the door is opened wide to potential discrimination against groups whom employers view as hard to train. The employer's arrangement of people according to personal, subjective assessment of trainability is a good example of Commons' rationing transaction.

For both the managerial and rationing transactions, the power of the employer is greater than the power of the employee. As a consequence, employees will want to convert such transactions to a final type—the bargaining transaction. "Bargaining transactions arise from the relations of those who are legally equal" (Commons 1961, 672). Collective action (through labor unions, for example) may be required for bargaining transactions to occur with employees finding a degree of legal equality through their collective bargaining agents. Antidiscrimination legislation may also be required to equalize the power of women and minorities waiting in queues to be admitted to private sector training and employment. In this case, government serves as the agent for the individual employee.

Notice how Commons has turned emphasis away from how human resources are allocated (efficiency) to how those same resources are utilized (along with issues of conflict, control, and social harmony). Economists had assumed that transactions would largely occur through markets, but according to Commons a large number of critical transactions occur outside the market. Managerial and rationing transactions within the firm imply inequality of power and the potential for exploitation of human resources—hence the justification for labor legislation that encourages bargaining transactions within business firms. The result of a bargaining transaction is reasonable value and not a market-determined price.

Commons and the Institutional Labor Economists

Commons' legacy is important for the study of unions and collective bargaining, but he wrote extensively about other institutions as well. He, in fact, did much to establish a second institutionalist tradition in the field of industrial relations—known as institutional labor economics. In this second tradition, reasonable value was also important, but in this case it was defined by the courts: "The courts generally go on the assumption that whatever is 'ordinary' is 'reasonable.' With them, 'customary' is *not* the *best practicable,* it is something of a *mean* between the palpably inefficient or stupid and the exceptionally capable and efficient" (Commons 1961, 860).

The history of development of industrial safety standards in Wisconsin demonstrates what Commons meant by the word reasonable. Commons argued for (and was able to achieve through the help of his students) a significant change in Wisconsin law regarding industrial safety. The law establishing the Industrial Commission in 1911 required that employers provide for their employees a level of safety that the nature and place of employment will reasonably permit. The precise level of safety required was interpreted to be at the mean between the highest and lowest levels of safety conceivably possible in a particular industry—a quite arbitrary and subjective definition. Commons and his students were able to change the definition to "the highest degree of accident prevention which is actually in practice by the best firms" in a particular industry (Commons 1961, 861).

The standard was objective since a search of the safety practices of all firms could readily produce the methods currently in use, and success in the marketplace (the ability to turn a profit) could identify the best firms. Commons referred to this approach as reasonably ideal, partly because the establishment of each new safety standard occurred through a committee of "employers, employees, and experts, having acquaintance with the best practicable methods and devices" (Commons 1961, 861). In fact, Commons considered it essential that institutions like the Wisconsin Industrial Commission contain representatives of opposing interests who would reach consensus on reasonableness. He referred to such institutional arrangements as "collectively practicable" (Commons 1961, 861).

Institutional Labor Economics
in an International World

Today, one could envision lawmakers in countries of the European Economic Community (EEC) or the North American Free Trade Agreement (NAFTA) operating in the same reasonably ideal manner exemplified by members of the Wisconsin Industrial Commission. Lawmakers would survey all the potential solutions for regulating workplaces in each of the member countries and pick the highest practicable level of protection. Note, however, that one assumes an economy in which a reasonable level of growth must also be achieved, and it may be difficult to determine what is reasonable growth. Despite this difficulty, institutional labor economists like Commons have, in the past, helped construct protective institutions that would reduce social risks and maintain a reasonable rate of economic growth. The European and U.S. versions of the welfare state, whose broad outlines were negotiated in the 1930s, were the result. New protective institutions will undoubtedly now need to be constructed for the EEC, NAFTA, and other regional trading areas.

In the United States, the best-known work of institutional labor economists has often coincided with periods of uneven or erratic rates of economic growth. Commons and his students were quite influential following the Great Depression, and other institutional labor economists were also influential in the 1960s. Several events coincided to make these periods extraordinarily good ones for institutionalist ideas. In the late 1960s, for example, the U.S. economy was growing quickly, but the rapid introduction of new technology and the need for highly trained workers in new industries meant that economic growth and employment security became interrelated issues. The main concern was for inflationary bottlenecks in training that could slow the overall rate of growth (Weintraub 1978). The emphasis thus shifted from the protective institutions of the post-depression era to institutions that would facilitate the transfer of resources from declining to growing sectors of the economy. The shift in emphasis of the 1960s is likely to be felt again now that regional trading blocs are being established.

In the 1960s, the Swedish tripartite labor market board—with representatives from labor, management, and government—was looked to as the ideal for creating the collectively practicable institutions advocated by Commons. In Sweden, a highly organized collective bargaining system complemented the achievement of collective objectives in other labor market institutions as well. A few national unions represented (and still represent) virtually all economic interests in Sweden. Furthermore, labor's goals were strongly supported by the Social Democratic Party which had held power in Sweden for decades. As a consequence, the tripartite Swedish labor market board could be given broad powers to facilitate the mobility of labor, to provide tax incentives for firms to relocate in regions of high unemployment, and to administer the Swedish system of unemployment insurance. A similar degree of collective representation in the administration of U.S. public training programs was, however, never achieved—although a number of attempts were made as the Manpower Development and Training Act (1962) was superseded by the Comprehensive Employment and Training Act (1973) and finally by the Job Training Partnership Act (1982). The difficulties in achieving a collective approach to training in the 1960s and 1970s are magnified when several countries are involved. A comparison of the experience in the 1960s with the experience in the 1930s may yield insight into the challenge of creating collectively practicable institutions across borders in the 1990s.

The U.S. piecemeal approach to training became most evident during President Johnson's War on Poverty in the late 1960s. This period differed significantly from the 1930s when Commons and his students combined their critique of economic theory with the practical task of legislating the Social Security Act. In the late 1960s, research on "manpower economics," like the War on Poverty that helped to support it, was not always well coordinated. McNulty, however, credits the work of institutions such as the Conservation of Human Resources program at Columbia University with helping to integrate disparate lines of research during this period by bringing together "not only labor economists but also labor sociologists, labor lawyers, political scientists, and other specialists in industrial relations" (McNulty 1980, 199). One could ask where similar work will now be done to bring together groups of people whose interests in labor market institutions are more international.

Dual roles were played by the institutional economists whose studies accompanied the government initiatives of the 1960s and 1970s. A number were asked to evaluate the effectiveness of a wide variety of governmental employment and training programs. Two factors greatly facilitated the evaluation research that ensued: (1) the development of human capital theory, dating from publication of Gary Becker's highly influential article in 1962 (Becker 1962), and (2) the rapidly growing capabilities for computer analysis of large volumes of survey data. The important role of evaluation research in the late 1960s was demonstrated in the opening chapter for the Industrial Relations Research Association's (IRRA's) annual research volume for 1969—a discussion by Cain and Hollister on the "Methodology of Evaluating Social Action Programs" (Cain and Hollister 1969).

A second important task was to analyze labor market institutions themselves, as exemplified in the work of Clark Kerr and E. Wight Bakke. Kerr emphasized the institutional rigidities (Balkanization) that existed from one local labor market to another, thereby demonstrating that government efforts to improve labor mobility might not be as easy as policymakers first thought. One of the most specific analyses of government training institutions was undertaken by E. Wight Bakke (1969) in which he contrasted the U.S. approach to employment and training programs with the approach taken by the Swedish labor market board. Clague and Kramer summarize Bakke's resulting critique: "Bakke's general criticisms were that manpower policy in the United States was: (1) overly concerned with the supply of labor and its placement and (2) overwhelmingly concerned with 'the most disadvantaged and poverty-stricken portion of that supply,' while it ignored the needs of other members of the labor force" (1976, 42).

Bakke observed that U.S. human resource policy was rarely synchronized with other macro-economic policies of the federal government and that little institutional structure existed through which such a coordinated approach could occur. Bakke's critique would be even more applicable today if applied to the member countries of NAFTA or the EEC.

Today, new opportunities for institutional analysis have arisen due to public concern for U.S. international competitiveness. Mangum's treatment of the U.S. system of employment and training institutions is a good example of renewed institutional interest. Mangum categorized all U.S. educational and training institutions in terms of the age and ability levels of their clientele. The main problem, viewed from the perspective of the nation as a whole, is the following: (1) to provide sufficient human capital to the economic system so that it will grow at a reasonably high rate, and (2) to facilitate an equitable and even movement of people through the system so that economic change will not leave people abandoned (the second chance training system). Mangum and others argued that facilitating the movement of people through the system was a lifelong process, "a process of becoming rather than a state of being" (Mangum 1989, 9).

In the domestic arena, U.S. institutional economists have studied the way that employment and training programs contribute to faster economic growth; in the international arena, a similar study has been made of the relationship between economic development and the rise of national labor movements. In 1964, Kerr, Dunlop, Harbison, and Myers published the results of their extensive study relating growth and change in labor movements to the process of industrialization. The convergence hypothesis was forcefully argued in their work—namely that industrialization, because of its common technological requirements, would create a relatively homogeneous work environment across countries of diverse cultural experience. As a consequence, industrial relations practices which, at first, might be strikingly different from country to country would converge, thus producing a common system of labor relations for all industrialized countries. At about the same time, Ross and Hartman (1960) argued that as countries aged, industrial relations practices would become increasingly routine, thus leading to the withering away of the strike as a dispute settlement mechanism. In the time period since each study was done, evidence in support of either hypothesis has been weak, thus strengthening the position of scholars who argue for the strong and pervasive influence of culture. If convergence is not likely, then how should collectively practicable institutions be built across borders?

Labor Market Institutions and Economic Development

The relationship between economic development and the growth of the labor movement has been a long-standing issue for all industrial relations scholars, not just institutionalist labor economists. Marx argued that a reformist labor movement could forestall but not prevent the collapse of the capitalist system. But Commons, in his well-known "Shoemakers" article, took issue with the Marxist contention that the aging system of capitalism, alone, changed relationships between employees and their bosses.

Commons argued that expansion of markets over wide geographical areas created a need for more standardized products which in turn created a need for the division of labor. The replacement of craft with factory production was the inevitable result, thereby changing the relationships between the newly established factory owners and their employees. Labor unions developed as a response to the job insecurity engendered by task specialization and the employer's ability to replace workers who had narrow, easily acquired skills. For Marx, the labor union was a temporary form of protection from capitalist exploitation; for Commons, the labor union could provide a permanent form of job protection as markets continued to expand. In Commons' view, unions would become less important only if markets and technology changed—making specialized products once again the rule.

When industrial relations scholars examine the historical process of economic development, the two institutionalist traditions initiated by Commons seem once again to become intertwined. What then is the major difference between the two traditions, at least as I have defined them here? This difference is simply that institutional labor economists have extended the Wisconsin School's more narrow focus on the labor movement to all of the societal institutions that offer protection from changes in markets and technology. For institutional labor economists, the process of economic growth and its effects are always close at hand. To be harmonized are the sharply conflicting interests of societal groups which are caught in the seemingly irreconcilable demands of economic change. Institutionalists of both schools of thought assume that markets alone will not harmonize economic interests. The institutions studied must therefore be designed to resolve conflict.

The Institutionalist Thought of John Dunlop

Perhaps one of the most influential works by an institutional labor economist was published in 1955—John Dunlop's *Industrial Relations Systems*. Although the term *institution* did not even appear in the index to this book, the approach was clearly institutionalist. Dunlop built his analysis on three main institutions (actors, as he prefers to call them): labor, management, and government. A fourth institution, the labor market, strongly affected the other three.

Dunlop subscribed to Talcott Parson's idea that stable relationships can exist over long periods of time among institutions connected to each other in a mutually reinforcing system. According to Dunlop, early in the process of industrialization a long-run pattern of relationships would be established for the main institutions that represented labor, management, and government. "The major characteristics of a national industrial-relations system appear to be established at a relatively early stage in the industrial development of a country, and in the absence of a violent revolution in the larger community, a national industrial-relations system appears to retain these characteristics despite subsequent evolution" (Dunlop 1958, 307).

Like other American institutionalists, Dunlop was not persuaded by the Marxist notion that the institutions of industrial society are in a process of constant change due to inherent contradictions within the system itself. The institutions of an industrial relations system could change, wrote Dunlop, but they would do so in response to changes in their environment, and there is certainly nothing automatic about such change. If anything, changes are apt to be temporary since the system has a built-in tendency to return to its original state. "The idea of an industrial-relations system implies a unity, an interdependence, and an internal balance which is likely to be restored if the system is displaced, provided there is no fundamental change in the actors, contexts or ideology. Industrial-relations systems show considerable tenacity and persistence" (Dunlop 1958, 27).

The key question in Dunlop's framework of analysis is how to determine when fundamental change has occurred, thereby signaling that the system is headed for a new internal balance with institutions adjusting accordingly. Dunlop is clear about where to look for fundamental change; unfortunately he is less clear in defining what degree of change should be considered fundamental. Institutions can be fundamentally changed if the technology of production or the rules of the market change significantly. Fundamental changes can also be the result of unexpected historical events. Change can be strongly affected by the sequence of historical events—whether social or political. Finally, the process of economic development and how it is controlled by elite groups within society can also produce fundamental and long-lasting changes in institutional relationships.

Dunlop presumed stability in the system of industrial relations and drew attention to the extraordinary events that upset the equilibrium of the system as it moved through time. But it is difficult to know in advance whether an observed change in technology, market rules, or history is sufficient to change the entire set of institutional relationships. Furthermore, Dunlop's systems analysis is perhaps uncomfortably close to the implicit systems analysis of classical economists who presumed that the economic system achieved equilibrium through the harmonizing capabilities of markets. Dunlop is much less clear about the mechanisms that keep the industrial relations system in a position of stability. He also does not analyze whether institutions could be constructed to change the entire system by releasing conflict and then reestablishing a new order. For Dunlop, change appears to occur from outside the system; institutions are conservative in that they seek to contain the changes and reestablish stability.

In Dunlop's analysis, the most confident prediction for the future is that the system will not change. Note, however, that in subsequent research, Dunlop and three co-authors (Kerr, Dunlop, Harbison, and Myers 1960) concluded that the influence of manufacturing technology on industrial relations was sufficient to override chance historical events and culture to create a convergence of systems (see the discussion above). In a follow-up study, (Dunlop et al. 1975), the four authors hedged on their earlier conclusions. In the latter work, the authors conceded that convergence may not have been as probable given the pervasive effects of culture. The two studies simply demonstrate the inherent difficulty in measurement—how much change is enough to be considered fundamental? This difficulty may be partly responsible for the more micro approach taken by industrial relations scholars in the 1970s and 1980s where individual behavior in the workplace was emphasized more than institutional analysis.

Labor-Management Cooperation and the Institutionalist Tradition

The recent attention given to cooperative labor-management relationships is an important exception to the above assertion that current analysis of individual behavior usually takes precedence over analysis of institutions. The new interest in cooperative relationships combines both of the two institutionalist traditions described above plus a third more recent line of thought. First, the Wisconsin School tradition has led some industrial relations scholars to analyze labor-management committees within a collective bargaining framework—asking how unions might deal with a broad range of issues not traditionally covered by the collective agreement. (An early example is Healy's (1965) analysis of the west coast mechanization and automation agreements in the shipping industry.) Bargaining theory helps to understand how joint committees can address difficult issues even in the context of an adversarial labor relations environment—issues pertaining to work climate, managerial authority, and employer/employee communications, for example (see Kochan et al. 1986).

A second way in which institutionalists have contributed to the topic of labor-management cooperation is through an analysis of area labor-management committees. Here the tradition represented by institutional labor economists provides the framework for analysis. Industrial cities have often established joint labor-management committees to improve the economic reputation of their communities, since a climate of industrial peace and joint labor-management cooperation is viewed as an important element in attracting development capital. The joint labor-management committee has no formal role in the private negotiations that take place between labor and management, but informally, committee members can introduce to otherwise private negotiations some sense of overall community interests. If successful, committee members can convert bilateral negotiations into tripartite discussions of the effects of peaceful dispute settlement on economic growth within the community.

The combination of objectives—economic growth and peaceful settlement of conflict over wages and working conditions—makes the study of industrywide labor-management committees a natural subject for research by institutional labor economists. In a recent study, Kochan, Katz, and McKersie report on two such committees—one in the retail food industry and one in clothing. In each, technological change has been the issue most likely to reveal the tension between economic growth and industrial conflict that emerges in joint committees. Concerning the Tailored Clothing Technology Corporation, Kochan says the following:

This project represents a dramatic example of a union, in this case the Amalgamated Clothing and Textile Workers Union (ACTWU), getting involved at a very early and basic stage in the research-and-development effort to mechanize the production of garments in order to help stem the flow of imported goods. . . . The ACTWU and the International Ladies Garment Workers Union (ILGWU) have been involved in strategic matters throughout the history of the garment and textile industries. . . . At the macro level of the industry, the unions have always wrestled with trade-offs between, for example, wage policies, imports, emerging non-union competition, and viability of the organized sector. . . . All of this can be seen as a form of private industrial policy. (Kochan et al. 1986, 187, 188)

Labor-Management Cooperation and the Problem of Agency

Kochan and his co-authors use the joint labor-management committees to illustrate the potential strategic role labor can play in long-run, industrywide policies. Interestingly though, joint committees serve as agents for both labor and management. Together they try to design solutions to conflict that will serve the interests of all constituents. Yet labor-management committees may not always be able to satisfy all constituents, and some are designed only to satisfy a given set of constituents. As a consequence, an institutional analysis of labor-management committees must take into account the kind of agency function that is to be performed. Industrial relations scholars who trace their intellectual roots to the Wisconsin School or to other institutional labor economists would tend to ask how the joint committee serves an agency function for individual employees. Scholars who feel more affinity to a third school of thought called neo-institutionalism would start with the assumption that the joint committee, in reality, serves an agency function for the firm's management.

In real life, joint labor-management committees do vary with regard to the agency function that they perform. Committees entitled "Quality of Work Life Committees" have typically tried to reconcile the interests of labor and management and to serve as an agent for both. Quality circles can perform the same function, but if these are simply a vehicle for passing on information to management with little autonomy to affect policy significantly then one should assume that the committee is acting as an agent for management.

When the quality circle acts as an agent for management, the problem is how to structure informal contractual agreements with employees so that, voluntarily, they will help improve group and individual productivity. Attention must be paid to individual job security and the power granted to employees to carry out productivity related suggestions. The structuring of such informal agreements (or implicit contracts) is the subject of a new institutionalist tradition that differs significantly from either of the older two institutionalist traditions associated with the field of industrial relations—neo-institutionalism. Neo-institutionalism is derived from neoclassical economics which emphasizes the efficient and rational economic behavior of individuals.

Some economic institutions (like quality of work life committees) have as their main purpose the harmonizing of actual or potential conflict between individuals or groups. If the conflict can be resolved or if a new order of interests can be created that eliminates the conflict then economic growth is facilitated. Institutionalists of the two older traditions outlined in this chapter (the Wisconsin School of industrial relations and institutional labor economists) have analyzed different institutions, but for both traditions the labor problem is the same—how to achieve a strong rate of economic growth and still guarantee a reasonable degree of economic security for the workplace. Scholars of both institutionalist traditions have dissented from main stream economics because these institutionalists assumed that competitive markets alone would not yield the harmony of interests required in industrial society.

The more recent scholars who call themselves neo-institutionalists are, however, not the same types of dissidents. Neo-institutionalists argue that institutional arrangements traditionally considered as alternatives to the market are really complementary to the market and serve to make it more efficient. The neo-institutional argument is probably best expressed through the work of Oliver Williamson.

Oliver Williamson and Neo-institutionalist Thought

In the older institutionalist tradition, the term *institution* was not used simply as a substitute for the word organization or group. If so, it would be hard to distinguish an institutional economist from a sociologist. Institutionalists focused their attention on organizations that were critical for resolving labor problems. For some, this meant analysis of labor unions; for others, it meant analysis of quality of work life committees, training organizations, or area labor-management committees. In the new institutionalist tradition, however, the term *institution* takes on a much broader meaning. In Oliver Williamson's recent book, *The Economic Institutions of Capitalism,* a bank, a food store, or a government-owned airline were all institutions. He used the term synonymously with firm or organization and argued that the tools of the neoclassical economist could be used to interpret the behavior of individuals in such institutions.

In the older institutionalist traditions, emphasis was placed on the nonmarket behavior of individuals as they sought to reconcile their conflicting interests with other groups in the economic system. Williamson, however, argued that apparent nonmarket behavior may really be quite rational and extend or complement the efficiency objectives of a system of market prices. It may appear, for example, that the main reason employees want unions is for the nonmarket function of raising wages above the prevailing market wage rate. In actual fact, however, unions may also serve the interests of their members for certain types of service. The union may help to evaluate complex wage and benefit packages for its membership, for instance. The union may also serve as a means of communicating to management the complex needs and preferences of its members. In either case, the union acts as an agent whose services both management and labor may value. The union, according to this view, is not so much a means for establishing reasonable value outside the marketplace as it is a market agent to be valued by its members because of the services it provides to employees and to management.[3]

Unions can also serve the efficiency objectives of a market system if a lack of information obscures the range of rational choices of individuals and if markets encourage opportunism.[4]

Protection against opportunism can be obtained through contracts—the costs of which are defined as transaction costs. According to Williamson, a primary objective for all institutions in a capitalist system is to minimize transaction costs. This economizing objective is often carried out through contractual arrangements.

When are contracts used and when are they unnecessary? Contracts are required if the parties to a contract must agree to share the use of an asset over time. Employee skills represent such an asset. With no uncertainty regarding how an employee's skills are to be developed, used, or lost to the firm over time, a contract could be designed which would (1) anticipate all potential future contingencies for the use of the shared asset, (2) assess penalties for violating agreements regarding how employee skills should be used, and (3) establish a means of enforcement for the contract. Williamson referred to this as a world of planning (1985, 31). Contracts are useful in this context if they accurately anticipate (plan for) the future and if they can be enforced.

If an employee has very little skill or if the skill possessed is generally applicable to a variety of firms, then no long-term contractual agreement is necessary since a continuous relationship between worker and firm is not highly valued by either party. "The employer can easily hire a substitute and the employee can move to alternative employment without loss of productive value. (This ignores transitional problems that may be associated with job relocation. All employees experience them, hence protection against arbitrary dismissal is sought. But the further question is what *additional* safeguards are warranted.)" (Williamson 1985, 242).

Contracts are desired in many actual employment situations because employees acquire skills that are specific to the firm, and a continuous employment relationship is therefore desirable. Despite the need for them, the contracts are hard to design due to uncertainty regarding future events. Under such circumstances, employers and employees develop what Williamson calls a "protective governance structure" (Williamson 1985, 243). Future contingencies are recognized in an often vaguely worded contract that is interpreted through daily negotiations between management and employee representatives. The vaguely worded contract in combination with the ongoing process of negotiation is one form of governance structure. In Williamson's view, the search for reasonable solutions to problems through daily negotiation minimizes transaction costs and therefore serves the efficiency objectives of management.

A contract signed collectively by a union and by management serves a variety of purposes—only one of which is efficiency. First, it may restrict the supply of labor, thereby raising wage rates—the monopoly face of unionism. Second, it may give voice to employee concerns—the political face of unionism. Finally, it may minimize transaction costs through a governance structure that protects each party to the contract from the potential opportunism of the other—the efficiency face of unionism. Giving voice to employee concerns and minimizing transaction costs would appear to be indistinguishable since they both occur through the same governance structure—usually some form of formalized grievance procedure. Williamson argued that the two quite different purposes served by unions could be distinguished, however, by analyzing the types of situations under which each occurred. By examining the contexts in which unionism occurred, a rough assessment could be made of the relative importance of efficiency or political objectives.

If one returns to the political scientist's view of what constitutes a governance structure, one would expect political activity wherever differences in values are resolved through appeal to legitimate authority. Williamson argued that if the political face of unionism was most important, then unions should be found wherever differences in values require resolution—in other words, fairly universally. But, at least in the United States, unions are not. If, on the other hand, serving efficiency interests is the most important function for unions, then they should be found in selected circumstances where contract costs are high—in other words, where employees have a high degree of firm-specific skill. Unions are more likely under such circumstances:

> Transaction cost analysis thus predicts that unions will arise early in such industries as railroads, where the skills are highly specific, and will arise late in such industries as migrant farm labor, where skills are nonspecific. It further predicts that the governance structure (job ladders, grievance procedures, pay scales) will be more fully elaborated in industries with greater specificity than in those with less (steel versus autos is an example). (Williamson 1985, 256)

For Williamson, job ladders, grievance procedures, and pay scales were the visible evidence of a firm's governance structure. But, as has been pointed out by political scientists, governance of any kind implies some system of authority within the firm. Williamson argued that under a capitalist form of production, the system of authority, and the employment contract were intertwined. The employer can follow a system of inside contracting whereby material, equipment, floor space, and capital are provided to subcontractors who hire their own employees and supervise production. Under such a system, the main employer has no need for a governance structure. But if the workers are hired directly by the main employer and not by the subcontractor, the issue of governance needs to be resolved. "The Authority Relation mode involves capitalist ownership of equipment and inventories coupled with an employment relationship between capitalist and worker. The employment relation is, by design, an incomplete form of contracting. Flexibility is featured as the employee stands ready to accept authority regarding work assignments provided only that the behavior called for falls within the 'zone of acceptance' of the contract" (Williamson 1985, 218).

Presumably, within the zone of acceptance that Williamson described, governance occurs either by managerial command, by democratic decisions of management and employees, or by some combination of the two. The labor union may choose to modify managerial authority to a lesser degree by establishing a grievance procedure through which managerial decisions can be challenged after the fact. Or the choice may be to challenge authority to a greater degree through democratic decision-making committees in which managerial proposals for future action must be submitted to a vote. In the United States, grievance procedures are the usual way of modifying managerial authority. In European countries, the company works council is often the chosen vehicle.

In the older institutional tradition as represented by Commons, unions were viewed as protective institutions that shielded their members from arbitrary managerial decisions. In other words, unions provided a countervailing power within the firm to rationalize the actions of management—forcing on them predictable and consistent rules. Through a process of negotiation, management and labor wrote rules that both judged to be reasonable. In short, collective negotiation occurred in response to the irrational, nonmarket behavior of management.

In the newer institutional tradition, as represented by Williamson, a governance structure comes about through individual, rational market behavior. In this case individuals agree to a quite limited form of participation in the decisions of the firm (governance) in exchange for protection of the skills that they acquire over the long term. Employees feel that they are an important part of the production process and therefore act as good agents for the employer by efficiently performing the firm's profit-making activities. In return, these employees gain long-term job security.

Employees have not gained their autonomy or job security collectively. The employer has granted these benefits because the production process or service that is provided requires it. Employees have not created one of Commons' collectively practicable institutions to bargain with the employer. Rather, the employer has voluntarily created a limited governance structure that helps employees feel involved. The governance structure could be seen as a subtle form of control created by the employer to solve the agency problem. In both the earlier and the latter institutional traditions, the end result is the same—a protective governance procedure. In the earlier tradition, though, the governance structure serves an agency function for employees. In the tradition of neo-institutionalism, governance serves an agency function for employers.

As noted in a previous chapter, political scientists had complained of an apparent contradiction in the governance of U.S. business enterprises. Stockholders are represented on the boards of directors of all firms, but employees only have access to a governance structure if the firm is unionized. If not unionized, employees have little choice but to leave the firm when they are unhappy with its operation. Why should stockholders have more claim to governance than employees? Do all employees have a right to governance? Should employees be represented on the board of directors? Williamson addresses all three questions by analyzing the firm's transaction costs.

For Williamson, stockholders lay claim to a governance structure—not because it is their right to do so, but because it makes sense economically. Dahl, in contrast, sees a contradiction when stockholders have a right to representative governance but do not have the power to control the day-to-day production process of management. The difference between Dahl and Williamson lies mainly in the purpose each ascribes to governance.

Dahl, the political scientist, assumed that governance was needed mainly to reconcile conflicts in values among the various members of an organization. Political activity or governance occurred as members of the organization appealed to their authorities to resolve differences over how production would be controlled. In short, conflict over the day-to-day control of production was the reason for governance. It is therefore contradictory to grant the firm's main governance rights to members who are farthest removed from conflicts over production—namely the stockholders.

Williamson, the economist, assumed that governance was needed when members of the organization ran large risks that their capital would be expropriated and when the risks could not be easily insured against loss through the usual method—enforceable contracts. Since an organization's constituents have varying amounts of capital invested in a firm (some through stocks and bonds, some through training) and bear variable risks of expropriation, governance should not be universally required. A governance structure would only be created, according to Williamson, when transaction costs were high (when it was difficult to specify anything more than a vaguely worded contract). Stockholders have developed a governance structure for themselves because they have so little control over the firm. Stockholders might prefer a detailed contract with upper-level management that spells out how the firm is to be run and how it will provide a high level of return to the stockholders' capital. But such a contract cannot be written. The next best alternative is a vaguely phrased understanding with upper-level management and a voting procedure for removing them from power if necessary.

For Williamson, the firm's board of directors is not an extension of a stockholder's property rights. It is an economic necessity. Whether employees should also have representation on the board is not so much a matter of their right to be heard; it is rather a question of whether they also are faced by uncontrollable economic circumstances that threaten their human capital. Sudden, unexpected, and uncontrollable competition that threatens to close plants in the meat packing or automobile industries, for example, could lead employees to want representation on the board of directors if (1) they had expected to work with the firm for a long time, (2) if they had acquired specific, nontransferable skills for which they were well paid, and (3) if they believed that board representation would protect against the threat. Under such circumstances, the board's governance procedures would serve as a substitute for the detailed contract that employees might prefer. Because of the radically different purposes served by the governance institutions described by Dahl and Williamson, the two scholars have hardly spoken the same language. Dahl defined governance as a continuous process of private government decision making. For Williamson governance was a discontinuous series of spot checks on power—a vote at the annual meeting of stockholders, a grievance, or a bargaining table proposal about relative salary levels. The not-very-democratic annual meeting of stockholders would meet Williamson's requirements for governance, whereas Dahl's ideal type might resemble a U.S. quality of work life committee or a German works council.

Neo-institutionalist thought is a far cry from the older institutionalist traditions of industrial relations. Neo-institutionalists are individualistic to the core. The protection they envision does not come so much from a collectivity (the labor union, for example) as it does from each contract that an employer holds with a single employee. When contracts can only be vague, implicit understandings, they are then supplemented by a governance structure that operates from time to time to protect the individual interests of employees or stockholders. The labor union as a collective agent of shared employee interests is replaced by the labor union as an agent for individual employee interests.

Institutionalist Thought:
European and American Contrasts

Institutionalist perspectives have been a strong influence on European as well as American industrial relations scholars. It is not the purpose of this book to present a truly international perspective on industrial relations thought—conveying the American perspective is difficult enough. Nevertheless, I will try to determine to what degree the American perspective, as represented first by Commons and more recently by Williamson, is unique or culture bound.

A European perspective on industrial relations starts with Karl Marx, and a key characteristic of Marxist thought is missing in much of American institutionalist thought—the concept of class. (Though it has been central to the analysis of a number of modern-day economists associated with the Union for Radical Political Economy.) Commons does not treat class as a critical variable in his analysis. In his famous "Shoemaker" article, class is used to describe groups of people who occupy various roles in the ongoing process of economic development. For example, the merchant capitalist or manufacturer class is distinguished from the wage-earner class (Commons 1913). But class structure is not the driving force that changes the relationship between one group of people and another as the economic system grows. Instead, the expansion of the market and accompanying changes in the technology and scale of production are what define and redefine the relationship between employers and employees. Economic and social classes exist but they have a relatively unimportant influence on industrial relations. "Marx's unyielding class struggle was fundamentally at odds with the core of Commons' thought and teaching which was that democratic institutions have the capacity to produce resolutions (note—not solutions) of conflict through due-process determinations of reasonableness . . . the class struggle can be 'reconciled in the public interest' without the triumph of one class over another" (Barbash 1967, 165).

European industrial relations scholars often reject the revolutionary Marxist's explanation for changes in the capitalist system over time, but they have also been more inclined than many American scholars to emphasize the role of class structure in affecting industrial relationships. A reformist European industrial relations tradition that also takes class structure into account is probably best exemplified by the work of Sidney and Beatrice Webb—industrial relations scholars who helped found the British Fabian Society, the British Labour Party, and the London School of Economics.

Though they rejected the Marxist philosophy of class struggle, the Webbs held strongly socialist views. The Fabian Society that the Webbs helped found in 1884 promoted economic equality and collective ownership of the country's resources. A number of influential persons in Britain helped advance the educational goals of the Fabian Society, which would eventually have affiliates throughout the country. The Society never became a political party per se, but it was to have a strong influence on the British Labour Party during its formative years early in the twentieth century. Sidney Webb was influential in both organizations and with the British dramatist, George Bernard Shaw, published *Fabian Essays* (1889)—a classic work in British socialist thought.

The Webbs' extensive study of British trade unionism should thus be viewed in the context of their socialist outlook. In their classic book, *Industrial Democracy* (1897), the Webbs argued that not only were trade unions compatible with democratic forms of government, they also contributed positively to the institutionalization of democracy. The Webbs observed that the important role of markets to send signals back and forth between buyers and sellers was often softened by a variety of institutional arrangements that protected the parties to a transaction. The discipline of the market was quite often too harsh for sellers who, as a consequence, set up a variety of protective institutions for themselves—of which the labor union was but one form. The Webbs went on to argue, however, that what began as a protective institution for working-class members of society, took on a more important role—the translation of the democratically expressed needs of the working class into administrative decisions:

If the democratic state is to attain its fullest and finest development, it is essential that the actual needs and desires of the human agents concerned should be the main considerations in determining the conditions of employment. Here, then, we find the special function of the Trade Union in the administration of industry. The simplest member of the working-class organization knows at any rate where the shoe pinches. The Trade Union official is specially selected by his fellow-workmen for his capacity to express the grievances from which they suffer, and is trained by his calling in devising remedies for them. (Webb and Webb 1897, 821)

If the governance structure of the labor union was initially a protective arrangement, it then soon became something else—a form of political governance quite close to the ideal type espoused by Dahl. The Webbs concluded their argument with policy implications for government: institutions that promote general welfare, efficiency, and industrial democracy should be encouraged while institutions that promote the opposite should be discouraged. Since unions have all three kinds of effects, they should be encouraged in those areas where their effects are positive, and the role of the academic is to identify such. This the Webbs did through extensive field work, interviewing, and analysis of the daily activities of trade unions.

For the Webbs, labor unions could serve a broader societal goal of strengthening workplace democracy—if only they were encouraged through public policy. This important belief of the Webbs is reflected in the public policy positions of socialists and social democrats throughout Europe today. The result is legally mandated works councils for all firms of a given size (whether unionized or not) in a variety of European countries.

More than anything, the link between the labor movement and the democratic control of production processes distinguishes European from current-day American institutional thought. Europeans are, in fact, much closer to traditional industrial relations thought in the United States than they are to neo-institutionalists. Barbash observes the following about Commons' more traditional institutionalist philosophy: "Commons' americanization of the labor movement consisted of: . . . formulating an intermediate ground of union and worker interest which rejected equally the atomized individualism of classical economics and the overarching class struggle of the socialists" (Barbash 1967, 161).

Most of today's European socialist labor leaders would agree with Commons. They reject class struggle and the extreme individualism implied in neo-institutionalist thought. Firm-level governance structures are encouraged, not solely where transaction costs are high, but universally throughout a more democratized industrial society.

Summary

The various traditions of institutional economics cover much ground. Institutionalists can be found at work analyzing topics in every one of the four major areas first spelled out in the model presented in this book's initial chapter. Yet some areas are dealt with more heavily than others. Institutional labor economists, for example, initiated their dissent from classical economics by arguing that processes of development can not be expected to occur automatically—even in a free-market economy. The entire path of economic development of a nation can not be expected to occur harmoniously just because a free market exists. Instead, strong conflicts over how development should occur can be negotiated through collective action, and reasonable solutions will sometimes take the place of market solutions in the development of human resources.

Institutional labor economists and neo-institutionalists alike have placed major stress on the maintenance of human resources. Institutional economists have focused much attention on collective methods to insure against societal risks. Commons and his students were heavily involved in the passage of social security legislation in the United States, for example. Institutionalists of the 1960s and 1970s analyzed employment and training programs for their effectiveness in achieving a rapid rate of growth in the U.S. economy and for maintaining reasonable economic security for individual workers. Today's institutionalists focus attention on joint labor-management committees, both in the firm and in local area labor markets, analyzing their ability to influence the nature of investment and to insure stable, long-term growth in employment opportunities.

Not all institutionalists are alike. The neo-institutionalist tradition reveals another split from the orthodoxy of neoclassical economics. Neo-institutionalists are weak dissidents from the neoclassical tradition, however. For these most recent institutionalists, a labor union is viewed as a logical extension of market forces. Where market contracts are difficult to construct and enforce (are costly), labor unions emerge—offering to supplement market forces with a limited form of governance for contracts over time. Governance, in this case, is adopted by individuals only to insure that the risks of investment of time and energy in learning new skills are minimized. The union is simply a necessary instrument for making market forces work, not an expression of alienation from work, of class interests, or even of workplace solidarity. The union does not consciously remove wages from competition or establish nonmarket value based on some commonly accepted evaluation of reasonableness.

Neo-institutionalists argue that unions will appear during the process of economic development when labor contracts are highly desirable, but costs of establishing such contracts are high. In other words, unions will most likely occur only under selective conditions—not universal ones. Older institutionalist traditions in the field of industrial relations view the union as only one institution involved in the continuing debate over how to control the rate and nature of economic development—in essence, a universal labor problem. Neo-institutionalists leave the problem of economic development to the market. For them there is no single labor problem. The main problem is efficiency (minimizing the costs of labor contracts), not security.

Finally, the European challenge is to take another step farther in thinking about labor problems. European institutionalists adopt the political scientist's viewpoint that the labor union is one way to change the authority structure of the firm. The Webbs argued that unions could be useful instruments—not simply for achieving contract efficiency, but for achieving a more democratic society. European institutionalists argue that unions should not be left to themselves either as market agents for their members or as forums for negotiating the day-to-day concerns of economic development and change. Rather, they should be encouraged to further the goals of a more democratic and more egalitarian society.

Chapter 6

THE PSYCHOLOGISTS AND INDUSTRIAL RELATIONS

Throughout this book, a knowledge of psychological theory has been implicit. In chapter 1, I quoted Polanyi's famous passage describing early industrial society as a "satanic mill." A system of uncontrolled markets was seen to have negative psychological effects on individuals—threatening them with death due to social exposure. Subsequent chapters described systems theorists, Marxist theorists, non-Marxist sociologists, and institutional economists in terms that were strongly psychological. For Marxists, the motivation to change the economic system lay in feelings of exploitation. Systems theory has undergirded my own depiction of industrial society as a continuous negotiation among powerful agents—each of whom can move the industrial relations system from one to another locus of control. But in this system, the force motivating individuals to seek out agents is a feeling—a feeling of insecurity that comes when the market is the locus of control, or a feeling of alienation that occurs when any one agent acts on its own interests and constrains the choices of the individuals it is supposed to represent. Institutional economists have examined the implications of the classical economists' presumption that a feeling of social harmony should accompany free-market economic development. Barbash states that trade unions in the west were born out of a sense of "outrage against capitalism's and industrialism's exploitation and alienation," but that outrage turned into negotiation as trade unions entered their modern phase (Barbash 1991, 347).

Kaufman argues that what sets industrial relations scholars apart from some other social scientists (neoclassical economists in particular) is their underlying model of human psychology:

Whatever the nature of the cause and effect relationship, intervening between stimulus and response is the 'psychological field' of each of the affected individuals—his or her attitudes, values, preferences, motives, perceptions, aspirations, and expectations. The causal path can be represented schematically as: Stimulus → (psychological field) → response.

Since industrial relations is concerned with human behavior in the context of the world of work, all industrial relations research that seeks to deduce or test 'If A then B' . . . must contain or be based on an underlying model of human psychology. This generalization is true not only of IR research that pertains to the behavior of individuals but also to [research] dealing with aggregate relationships or the behavior of institutions. . . . Economic research typically . . . minimizes the role of psychological variables or processes as determinants of IR outcomes. Research by scholars in personnel, organizational behavior, and sociology, on the other hand, generally gives much greater weight to these factors. (Kaufman 1989, 73, 74)

In this chapter, I examine the important contributions of psychologists, social psychologists, and students of personnel (human resource management). In an earlier chapter, the sharp difference between Marxist and non-Marxist industrial relations scholars was referred to as a great divide. Yet another great divide is addressed here—namely the difference in perspective that occurs when industrial relations theory is derived from an individual rather than a workplace or societal perspective. To this point, labor problems have been framed in societal or institutional contexts: the Marxist's problem of class conflict and exploitation or the institutionalist's problem of achieving rapid economic growth with reasonable job security. But, as noted in chapter 2, a single, all encompassing labor problem becomes redefined when viewed from the individual's perspective—a whole series of labor problems take its place.

Individual attitudes, aspirations, motivations, and needs as expressed in industrial workplaces are a significant part of the world of the psychologist (Dunnette 1976). The set of feelings about work can be positive and contribute to an individual's sense of self-efficacy (Bandura 1977) and usefulness to society, but feelings can also be negative, resulting in a strong sense of alienation from work or from the social system that defines work roles (Seeman 1975). If a psychologist were to point to a single overarching labor problem (rather than many individual problems), it might be how an individual worker seeks to avoid alienation in work.[1]

As defined above, the labor problem might appear trivial since the simplest way to avoid alienation in work is not to work at all. An economist can salvage this debate easily, however, by arguing that work is not simply a matter of fulfilling psychological needs but, more often than not, a necessity—a means for survival. From a combined economic and psychological perspective, the labor problem may thus entail a series of decisions and tradeoffs: how to satisfy one's psychological needs for satisfaction and fulfillment in work, while at the same time satisfying economic needs for income and job security. Seen in a different way, one might argue that individuals make tradeoffs in an orderly way.

Maslowe's famous hierarchy predicts the order: basic/physiological, safety/security, belonging, esteem, and self-actualization (Maslowe 1970).

As before, industrial relations scholars do not view industrial society benignly. Rather, industrial society is problematic: it involves conflict—sometimes violent—and hard choices which imply difficult decisions about several socially desirable outcomes. Psychologists and economists may not all necessarily share the problematic view of the world of industrial relations scholars, however. And if they do not then there can be little overlap between the fields of psychology and industrial relations. In fact, however, the worlds of psychologists and industrial relations scholars do overlap. To see how, one must revisit the world of economics—neoclassical economics in particular.

Neoclassical labor economists have devoted much time to the labor problem as seen through the eyes of an individual. But for such economists, the term *labor problem* is itself problematic. In a world where the market is the main locus of control, the problem confronting an individual is mainly one of choice, and having choices is more opportunity than problem. Individuals must first sort out their own preferences for paid employment. Then they must review the market's information about the choices available and the benefit each choice will yield. Finally, they must choose. If there is a problem, it is in obtaining good information and matching available jobs with individual preferences. When a wide variety of jobs are available and are well advertised, choosing among them can hardly be called the labor problem. Individuals simply select those jobs that best meet their particular economic and psychological needs.

From an individual perspective, problems develop only when choices are restricted or controlled—something the neoclassical economist resists assuming. Perlman, in his classic work, examines the effect on worker attitudes and behavior that occurs when a psychology of scarcity prevails, rather than a psychology of opportunity (Perlman 1949). He argues that most employees will assume that job opportunities are scarce. A worker's choices in the external labor market can easily become controlled (see Schwab, Rynes, and Aldag 1987). The local, geographic nature of most labor markets controls choices. Discrimination, which assigns only certain categories of jobs to certain kinds of individuals, controls choices. And professional associations or craft unions may control choices by restricting the number who enter selected occupations.

The workplace itself may be a source of control—particularly if an individual's access to the labor market is restricted once employed. An employee who enters into a long-term employment contract, for example, will gain much in future job security, but if all employers hire only for entry-level positions, an employee's future access to the labor market (ability to quit and get another comparable job) will be sharply controlled (Osterman 1988). Furthermore, limited access to the labor market introduces the prospect of additional controls. In exchange for the long-term employment guarantee, an employer will often obtain strong rights to control human resources within the firm—to plan for their use, to transfer them from place to place, to retrain and redeploy them at will, and to control the organization's incentives which both motivate people to work and influence their attitudes toward the work itself (Begin 1991; Mintzberg 1983). From a worker's point of view, jobs may often be viewed as scarce and those that do exist are often subject to numerous controls. The industrial relations scholar who takes an individual perspective must therefore study the processes of control and countercontrol both in the labor market and in the firm. It is here that industrial relations, psychology, and economics are joined.

The Control Mechanism—One Important Link
Between Industrial Relations Scholars
and Industrial Psychologists

Several kinds of control and countercontrol could be discussed in this chapter: class control, negotiated forms of workplace control, and the more subtle controls of technology and its management. Marx believed that privileged members of society (the owners of capital) imposed controls on other social classes as a way of maintaining their privileged status. Commons, in contrast, thought that the impersonal forces of the market were more important than class influence and power—emphasizing the utility of negotiating reasonable rules to complement the dictates of the market. The societal control perspectives of both Marx and Commons have been presented in previous chapters; the main subject here is how technology and its management controls individuals in their local workplace environments.

Control is a concept important to industrial relations scholars but one that has quite different connotations depending on who or what is thought to be controlled.[2] The idea of control links the work of psychologists with that of other industrial relations scholars since the degree of control or autonomy that workers have over their own work is, in turn, constrained by the control of other members of complex organizations and by industrial society as a whole. Furthermore, the degree of control exercised by the broader social system can have a significant impact on the feelings workers have about their jobs and the fulfillment they may or may not derive from work.

Individual Attitudes, Control Mechanisms, and Organizational Efficiency: A Second Link between Industrial Relations Scholars and Industrial Psychologists

Industrial psychologists will often link individual attitudes and motivation (job satisfaction, feelings of equity with regard to pay and other rewards, and feelings of justice or injustice about the day-to-day practice of management) to the efficiency of organizations—in a business context, the productivity of the firm.[3] Though the degree of control that an individual has in an organization tends to be more important for an industrial relations scholar than organizational efficiency, firm-level productivity is nevertheless an issue well examined in the industrial relations literature (Ichniowski 1986; Kaufman 1992). The most salient question is whether collective bargaining, grievance procedures, and the system of controls established by unions make a firm more or less productive (Peterson 1990). An answer to the question requires an understanding of all the behavioral sciences previously examined—psychology, economics, political science, and sociology.

Given these broad areas of overlap between the fields of psychology and industrial relations, this chapter will be directed to the following specific topics: (1) the control and countercontrol structure of the firm and its effect on workers' individual attitudes, (2) the attitudes workers bring to their jobs and have toward others in a work organization, and (3) the link between work attitudes and the firm's productivity. Together, these topics lead to a set of labor problems that accompany the psychological work lives of individuals.

The Hawthorne Studies, Worker Attitudes, and Workplace Control

The previous chapter showed how beliefs about control over the economic system were root causes for disagreement between industrial relations scholars and classical economists. Industrial relations scholars disagreed with classical economists by asserting that a more harmonious work environment must be created through negotiations between worker representatives and the representatives of management or government. One should not assume that societal norms would automatically create the required harmonious environment for work.

In this chapter, beliefs about control over the business firm have created considerable disagreement between industrial relations scholars and industrial psychologists. Industrial relations scholars have disagreed with industrial psychologists when the latter assumed that a harmonious working environment could be engineered by proper management of individuals and their work environment. The disagreement was sharpest—at least in the United States—during the 1920s and 1930s when Elton Mayo and his followers applied the results of a series of experiments at Western Electric (the Hawthorne Studies) to their own formulation of the labor problem. Mayo's interpretation of the experiment's results (known as the Hawthorne effect) was that friendly interest in the work done by women in the bank wiring room led to higher productivity. Mayo and his followers devised a set of suggestions for how to manage labor problems in a humane way that was ultimately to become known as the human relations school—a movement that would collide with several basic assumptions of industrial relations scholars of the same time period. The disagreement can best be seen by comparing the assumptions of psychologists like Elton Mayo with the assumptions of economists like Commons and Perlman.

Both Commons and Perlman believed that a lack of harmony between labor and management was normal and not necessarily dysfunctional. The conflict could be resolved, if only temporarily, through negotiation. In contrast, Mayo and his followers assumed a natural community of interest between worker and manager (Bendix and Fisher 1961, 123)—an assumption that was attractive to management but ultimately was to be challenged by organized labor.

The gulf that grew up between psychologists of the human relations school and industrial relations practitioners (union leaders in particular) was wide and deep. It was well described by two psychologists writing about a decade ago. Gordon and Nurick (1981, 294) observed that American union leaders ultimately came to "consider psychology [as] just another tool of the clever manager." Some of the same kind of suspicion is sometimes now directed at persons trained in human resource management (HRM). The tension appears to center on whether psychological theory mainly teaches students of human resource management how to manipulate and control the work environment or whether negotiation, consensus building, and conflict resolution can also be derived from the psychological theory that underlies HRM. Mayo and his followers may have set the stage for HRM, but the question today is whether the props can and should be rearranged.

William Foote Whyte, an industrial relations scholar deeply involved in the early years of the human relations movement, argued that the gulf between human relations and industrial relations (and as a corollary the tension between HRM and industrial relations) was unnecessary. He believed that it stemmed from Mayo's early and unfortunate misinterpretation of the implications of the Hawthorne experiments. Whyte (1987) pointed out that in the famous bank wiring room experiment,[4] the women who worked there were not the only ones to be treated with caring management. A group of men was also provided with a friendly and sympathetic observer, but their productivity did not increase (showed no Hawthorne effect). Whyte believed that the reason was due to the way the work group was structured. The women were organized into what would now be called an autonomous work group where the control of management was significantly reduced. The men were not so autonomous:

> The hypothesis of the Hawthorne effect to explain the results of the test room study was attractive to [Mayo] because it fitted in with his previously stated convictions that the human problems of industry arose out of boredom and obsessive reveries suffered by workers in repetitive jobs. The company and the workers, he believed, would benefit by the establishment of a personnel counseling program to enable individuals to achieve catharsis by unburdening themselves to a sympathetic non-directive interviewer. (Whyte 1987, 488)

Mayo's solution to the psychological problems of the workplace was a paternalistic one initiated by management. His solution implied manipulation and control over the workforce through psychological means—a clever management tool. In contrast, American labor leaders and industrial relations scholars alike believed that although workplace problems could be converted to some degree of collaboration, it should be done by jointly negotiating the rules for managerial control. Both workers and management would thus have voice in creating a favorable, more harmonious workplace environment—a theme that would be taken up later by others (Hirschman 1970; Lewicki and Litterer 1985).

Mayo's interpretation of the Hawthorne experiments was not necessarily representative of other psychological theories that would ultimately be applied to the workplace. An important case in point is behaviorism initiated by the psychologist B. F. Skinner. Skinner wrote that "all control is reciprocal, and an interchange between control and countercontrol is essential to the evolution of a culture" (Skinner 1971, 174). The ideas of industrial relations scholars like Commons and Perlman are quite consistent with Skinner's in that they viewed union-management negotiation as a way to create a negotiated work culture within the firm. They agreed with Skinner that the interaction of managerial control and employee countercontrol was a prerequisite for changes in the culture over time—a position that was quite the opposite of the paternalistic approach recommended by Mayo.

Whyte believed that Mayo's influence delayed, for almost two decades, research on the effects of close supervision on productivity. In other words, an undue emphasis on individual attitudes toward work may have caused researchers to overlook the interaction of individual attitudes and organizational work structures. Today's industrial relations research on autonomous work groups and worker participation (for example, Verma and McKersie 1987; Osterman 1994) combines analysis of individual attitudes with an examination of changes in how organizations are structured—a social-psychological approach to the problems of workplace productivity that Whyte believed was appropriate. Not all psychologists have subscribed to the human relations school's assumption of a community of interest between labor and management—either at the time Elton Mayo wrote or now. Today's psychologists, for example, can be found investigating the processes of conflict negotiation, mediation, and grievance resolution (Lewicki 1986). Yet some industrial relations scholars and labor leaders continue to view the field of psychology with suspicion—perhaps due to the psychologist's ongoing interest in the control mechanisms of economic enterprises. To understand why the analysis of control mechanisms has provoked both suspicion and sharp debate, I begin with an analysis of Frederick Taylor's influential movement—scientific management.

Scientific Management and the Control/ Countercontrol Structure of the Firm

The contributions of Frederick Taylor to the whole of management thought have been well documented by numerous others.[5] For the field of industrial relations, Taylor's focus on the rationalization of production is particularly important:

> Taylor . . . divided jobs into their smallest constituent elements and worked out precisely what kinds of body movements were required by able workmen to execute individual tasks in the shortest possible time without increasing the intensity of labour. Similar tests were carried out to determine the most suitable equipment for each physical action and how the environment should be laid out to contribute to efficient and effective performance. This aspect of Taylor's system can be referred to as the rationalization of the technical preconditions of work. (Lane 1989, 119)

Superficially, Taylorism was a systematic way to achieve greater engineering efficiency in the flow of materials through the plant. But Taylorism also implied a change in managerial control over the workforce. Taylor argued that the rationalization of work should be done by technical experts so that not even management would ultimately control the work process. Rather, a scientific examination of alternative organizations of work would reveal which method was most efficient. According to Taylor, little argument could be made with the experts who recommended the introduction of specific work methods. A proper understanding of the technology of production would, in and of itself, produce harmony.

The introduction of scientific management in actual firms was not necessarily harmonious (Aitken 1960)—and the work of both psychologists and sociologists is helpful for interpreting why. For some sociologists, Taylor, like Mayo, failed to recognize the importance of organizational design on the feelings of individual employees and on workplace productivity: "For a number of theorists, notably Edwards, Burawoy and Friedman, the main constraint on scientific management is its rigidity. The attempt to create a managerial 'monopoly of conception' runs against a parallel requirement for some level of creative participation of shop floor workers to keep production going" (Thompson 1989, 133).

Radical industrial relations scholars might argue, in fact, that complete worker control over production results in the best production system. But for psychologists, who is in control is less important than the type of control that is exercised. Skinner believed that an excessive emphasis on autonomy (such as espoused by radical industrial relations scholars) could actually lead to an inaccurate conception of social control: "The literature of freedom has encouraged escape from or attack upon all controllers. It has done so by making any indication of control aversive. Those who manipulate human behavior are said to be evil men, necessarily bent on exploitation. Control is clearly the opposite of freedom, and if freedom is good, control must be bad" (Skinner 1971, 38).

For Skinner, the main objection to scientific management is not that managers trained in time and motion studies are "evil" people imposing exploitive controls on the workforce. People who work in modern industrial enterprises will be controlled by the environment in which they work—time and motion experts, or not. Scientific management is objectionable if the types of control that are devised are aversive: "The problem is to free men, not from control, but from certain kinds of control. . . . To make the social environment as free as possible of aversive stimuli we do not need to destroy that environment or escape from it; we need to redesign it" (Skinner 1971, 39).

Someone must design the nonaversive stimuli Skinner advocated, and here is where industrial relations scholars often part company with Taylor. Neoclassical economists, Commons, and Marx all hoped that the work environment could be redesigned, and all hoped that a greater degree of social harmony would be achieved in the process. But Taylor was alone in his belief that the redesign should be done by technical experts, and for that reason scientific management was and continues to be a subject of controversy.

The Control of Human Resources

Scientific management has been important for the field of industrial relations, in part, for the controversy it initiated both over control mechanisms and over who should be charged with designing (or redesigning) them. But Taylorism has also been important for a less direct reason. Scientific management was but one of a number of concurrent reforms in the technology of management that were initiated in the early part of this century—and then elaborated and extended. These managerial reforms shared with scientific management the intent to rationalize the technical preconditions of work. These reforms have had a strong impact both on the individual's own formulation of the labor problem and the industrial relations scholar's interpretation of it.

The creation of today's professional managers trained in human resource management is one of the more visible signs of the rationalization of the technical preconditions of work, but it is only one of a number of innovations that have occurred. A comparison of managerial responsibility and outlook toward the workforce at three disparate points in time reveals how the rationalization process occurred.

If the starting point is the year 1920, one finds that the personnel functions of nearly all large manufacturing firms would include job analysis, time and motion studies, systematic procedures for recruiting, screening, and selecting new employees, health and safety programs and training programs.[6] Employers would also usually provide lunch rooms, rest areas, recreational programs, and housing programs for employees. The rationalization of the personnel function was based mainly on things to be provided for employees.

By 1950, however, the revolution in thinking initiated by the Hawthorne Studies was clearly evident in the tasks assumed by increasingly rationalized personnel departments. Rather than concentrate on things, personnel managers were more concerned with the human side of the enterprise. Employee attitude surveys were very much in vogue—sometimes used to pinpoint employee needs and at other times used to indicate organizational weaknesses that might be exploited by the rapidly growing labor unions (Jacoby 1988b). Much attention was paid to factors of morale. The author of a personnel text of the time summarizes some of the thinking that lay behind these human innovations:

Modern industry requires that its personnel be not only technically competent to do the various jobs assigned to it, but capable of working in harness and harmony with other workers, willing to follow instructions and accept supervision. The program for obtaining such men [sic] calls for scientific recruiting and selection, and adequate training after hiring, good discipline, and other qualities. But what is becoming more urgent is that these men be conditioned in the larger aspects and interests of the industrial society as a whole. (Gilbertson 1950, 35)

The rationalization process was also reflected in the systematic ways in which managers were being trained. Managers were recruited from schools with newly developed masters in business administration programs and hired into management training programs. Once hired, managers would be evaluated through new, more elaborate appraisal systems. Finally, longer tenured managers were sent to a number of advanced management programs taught by faculty members at major universities.

Thirty years later in 1980, the most striking factor was the increased complexity of the personnel function. In part, this complexity reflected the increased complexity of organizational structures within which the personnel function operated. Gigantic U.S. corporations like Coca-Cola, General Electric, Phillip Morris, and USX defied a single set of rationalized personnel policies. Government regulations required that firms recognize the complexity of the workforce—the varying ages, genders, and races that comprise it. Individualized employee-benefit plans, employee-assistance plans, and various forms of profit sharing were often administered by the personnel departments of large firms. In 1980, personnel managers were not only asked to rationalize the various programs and benefits for employees, but also to assist top management in preparing a rationalized strategy for the firm as a whole, including conscious choices regarding the utilization of the entire workforce. As a result, many personnel departments changed their names to departments of human resource management.

Today's strategic human resource management plan for a complex firm is a far cry from the original time and motion studies advocated by Taylor. Hirschhorn (1984) argued that changes in the physical technology of the firm opened up new possibilities for organizing production. These in turn set in motion a process of rationalization—choices are made among the several possibilities that exist with the best options incorporated into the institutional structure of the firm. Over time the processes thus become routine. The rationalization of the technical side of the firm becomes reflected in the rationalization of the human side as well.

But where are the attitudes, opinions, and desires of individual workers as rationalization takes place? If Taylor's experts produced the technical design for production and if human resource professionals produced the design for the motivation, development, and utilization of the workforce, it might seem that the individual worker's view of labor problems was bypassed altogether. The rationalization process would have produced efficient, harmonious work processes—both for the technical and for the human side of the firm. At this point, the industrial relations scholar objects, arguing that the rationalization process itself may lead to louder demands for a voice in the establishment of work rules and in the choice of employee benefits. In practical fact, neither the time and motion expert nor the line manager can wish away the reactions of employees to the rationalization process. In a particularly severe form, the reaction to rationalization may be manifest in worker alienation.

Individual Attitudes Toward Work:
The Problem of Alienation

The practice of management is part of the firm's technology, and the reaction to managerial technology is an important area of study in industrial relations. But this concern is not new. Marx, for example, argued that a very strong worker reaction—alienation—was the direct result of the division of labor initiated by capitalists. Subsequent to Marx, numerous scholars have devoted much time and attention to the study of alienation—how best to define it, how to measure it, and how to identify its causes.

Alienation, a term generally used by sociologists and social psychologists, carries with it a wide variety of connotations, but Seeman identified six varieties as follows:

(a) powerlessness—the sense of low control vs mastery over events; (b) meaninglessness—the sense of incomprehensibility vs understanding of personal and social affairs; (c) normlessness—high expectancies for (or commitment to) socially unapproved means vs conventional means for the achievement of given goals; (d) cultural estrangement (called "value isolation") . . . —the individual's rejection of commonly held values in the society (or subsector) vs commitment to the going group standards; (e) self-estrangement—the individual's engagement in activities that are not intrinsically rewarding vs involvement in a task or activity for its own sake; and (f) social isolation—the sense of exclusion or rejection vs social acceptance. (Seeman 1975, 93, 94)

For the psychologist, the concept of alienation is often replaced with job dissatisfaction and its opposite—job satisfaction (Locke 1976). Both concepts are far less encompassing than the oftentimes broader societal idea of alienation, but like alienation, job dissatisfaction is also linked to the firm's technology, its mode of management, and its machinery. Job dissatisfaction as a reaction to particular kinds of industrial technology is one of many individual labor problems studied by psychologists. Psychologists have, for example, linked job dissatisfaction to characteristics of jobs that may, by their nature, decrease satisfaction (Hackman and Oldham 1975). Highly repetitive jobs with little autonomy may contribute to a sense of powerlessness, meaninglessness, self-estrangement, or social isolation. Psychologists, through expectancy theory (Vroom 1964; Porter and Lawler 1968), equity theory (Adams 1965), and theories of justice (Greenberg 1992) have also linked job dissatisfaction to the ways in which management establishes the reward systems of organizations (Ballou and Podgursky 1993), the ability of employees to complain about their work

(Miceli, Near, and Schwenk 1991), and reactions to two-tier wage plans (Capelli and Sherer 1990).

A Framework to Unify the Diverse Problems
Individuals Confront in the Workplace

The application of psychology to the workplace results in a wide diversity of individual problems: feelings such as inequity, injustice, job dissatisfaction, alienation, desire for autonomy, and resistance to control. No single labor problem seems to prevail. Yet a more unified view of the series of problems individuals confront is possible if the approach taken is more historical. Changes in the technology of production over time have, more often than not, invoked strong psychological reactions. A change in technology sets in motion a powerful set of forces affecting the social climate in which production occurs. This in turn affects the structure of individual rewards and production controls within the firm—often requiring individual employees to change their psychological expectations and behavior quite significantly. Psychology contributes significantly to industrial relations through its analysis of how individuals have adapted to and resisted these changes.

The first dramatic technological change of interest to industrial relations scholars was the industrial revolution. The shift from agricultural to industrial production must have caused serious problems for people accustomed to a secure feudal system. Psychologists were not on the scene to record and analyze the effects, but, as noted in the first chapter, the historian Polanyi has argued from a psychological perspective that the insecurity of market forces during the shift made a completely free-market system in subsequent time periods totally unacceptable. Individuals simply could not and would not withstand the personal insecurity.

A more recent dramatic shift in technology occurred during psychology's relatively short lifetime—a shift that many are still seeking to understand. Hirschhorn argued that the key factor in the shift was the change from steam- to electric-powered machinery. Under steam-powered machinery, factory production was constrained by the central drive shaft required to power a variety of machines geared to the central power source. But with the advent of electrical power, machines were uncoupled from the central drive shaft, and the entire organization of production was ready for change. Frederick Taylor was the first to recognize the possibilities for the reorganization of production and the subsequent rationalization process. The assembly line was to be the result of such rationalization.

From the individual's perspective, the assembly line represents much that is particularly problematic about industrial technology—at least since the in-

dustrial revolution. Assembly-line technology, by its standardization, work sim-
plification, and controls, reduces individual autonomy. This technology can also
lead to tedious, repetitive, and boring work. Finally, if skill levels are reduced,
assembly-line technology may also lead to a high degree of insecurity when
workers become more or less interchangeable parts of the production process.
The individual's labor problem became how to avoid tightly controlled, boring,
unchallenging work and, at the same time, retain long-term employment security.

Today yet another dramatic shift in technology is occurring that is affecting both the organization of production and individual reactions to it—computerization. Without a historical perspective on the change, one cannot be
certain how dramatic it has been or understand its full implications. Hirschhorn
speculates, however, that computerization is producing changes equally as profound as those that accompanied the shift from steam to electricity—that computerization is weakening the importance of assembly-line processes through
efficient decentralization of the firm's operations. Computers permit a further
uncoupling of production processes since they allow firms to decentralize the
information necessary for efficient production. The information itself can, in
fact, be viewed as the new power source for the firm by overshadowing the old
power source—electricity—since computers require relatively small amounts
of electrical energy for their operation.[7]

Changes in today's technology have set in motion forces similar to those
that accompanied the change from steam to electricity. Today, as before, technical experts are giving advice on how to rationalize the production possibilities
accompanying computerization. As in Taylor's time, industrial psychologists
are becoming involved in the problems of individual productivity and adjustment to the new technology. Quality circles and participative management are
being studied extensively, and in such studies, the firm's power source—information—is often crucial to the analysis.

Change in technology over time is an important dynamic that brings psychological theory to bear on the problems of industrial life—but it is not the
only one. Industrial life is also affected by the myriad of problems that arise
out of interpersonal relationships. The relationships would not be problematic
if one could assume that human beings had natural tendencies for harmony
and respect. But one cannot easily make such an assumption. The well-known
author and former chair of the Department of Psychology at the University of
Chicago put it as follows: "One feature that distinguishes humans from other
animals—perhaps as characteristic as speech or upright posture—is the fact
that we find so many ways to oppress and exploit one another. . . . 'Power' is
the generic term to describe the ability of a person to have others expend their
lives to satisfy his or her goals. . . . When there are great differences in power,

exploitation takes place even when people have the best of intentions" (Csikszentmihalyi 1993, 89).

Hoyt Wheeler speculated that the conflict that has been so characteristic of industrial life may originate in an innate, biological tendency toward aggression (Wheeler 1985). Certainly industrial life has created great differences in power, thereby opening the door to considerable exploitation. In this case, as in the case of technological change, the reactions of individuals are often a combination of individual sentiment and group behavior that fit well within the theoretical framework developed in this book.

The combined impact of technological change and increased opportunity for exploitation may lead to feelings of resentment, alienation, anger, and fear. If the feelings are strong enough (outrage, as Barbash describes it), a union, some other protective institution or some set of protective regulations may be demanded. The ideal institutional form would be one that is capable of reducing power differences, restoring some sense of autonomy and control over an individual's work life, and giving voice to individual grievances. A labor union is one such institution. But note that the union, if it is to be successful, must not begin to engender similar feelings of resentment, alienation, anger, and fear among its members. If so, these members will seek additional protection through other institutions or regulations.

Psychological theory provides the explanation for the underlying dynamic of the theoretical framework created here. Individuals resist allowing any one center of control to dominate their work lives—not the government, the business firm, the labor union, or the market. A concentration of power in any of these centers of control is unacceptable because of the potential for exploitation. It is unacceptable in the case of the market or the firm which relies on assembly-line technology because of the high degree of economic insecurity that results from the process of rationalization. A perfectly functioning (highly rationalized) marketplace would require instant individual accommodation to all types of technological change; human beings cannot adjust so rapidly.

The dynamics of my framework began with the construction of a rationalized system of prices and trade—the market. This in turn led to a psychological reaction in the form of feelings of alienation and insecurity. As a result, government protective policies, labor unions, and internal labor markets within large firms were built. As new centers of control became important, new psychological reactions occurred. In all cases industrial relations researchers have been preoccupied with documenting the influence of individual sentiment and group behavior on the changing structure of the industrial relations system, as well as the reverse effect of technological and institutional change on individual sentiment and group behavior.

Psychological Interpretations of
Collective Responses to Technological Change

If the reactions to changes in technology over time were only individual, the field of industrial psychology might possibly have developed with little or no connection to the field of industrial relations. But, in fact, reactions to changes in technology have been a combination of individual sentiment and group behavior. A full understanding of either reaction is not complete without the other—bringing both the fields of psychology and industrial relations more closely together.

A cursory review of industrial relations journals shows a wide variety of psychological research directed at the workplace problems examined above. In the last five years, for example, the *Industrial and Labor Relations Review* has reported on research that deals with the following issues: the connections between individual attitudes and voting behavior in union certification elections (Montgomery 1989; Schur and Kruse, 1992), the reasons for union members to feel satisfied with or committed to their unions (Kuruvilla, Gallagher, and Wetzel 1993), the variations in support among members for converting an employees' association into a labor union (Cornfield 1991), the attitudes of teachers toward merit pay (Ballou and Podgursky 1993), and the effects of worker morale on company productivity (Straka 1993). The last three annual research volumes for the Industrial Relations Research Association report on studies linking union beliefs to the probability of unionization (Wheeler and McClendon 1991), research linking union members' attitudes with participation in union affairs (Gallagher and Strauss 1991), an analysis of the weakening preferences of American workers for unionization (Farber and Kreuger 1993), and studies of unions as vehicles for democratic voice (Greenfield and Pleasure 1993).

In all of the studies cited above, changes in individual feelings are linked to subsequent collective action. Psychological theory, in effect, helps in understanding the preconditions for individuals to select agents to represent their interests. It also helps in understanding why agents will sometimes have difficulty in representing their members' interests and why members will at times become disillusioned with the agents they select.

The disillusionment that many individuals have felt regarding free-market systems, labor unions, government protective agencies, and large, powerful firms become more understandable when one recognizes the potential that each system has to restrict autonomy or to exploit individual energies, capabilities, and skills. The search for protection from such exploitation is the explanation for changes in the transactions that individuals make with their agents over time. And by understanding this dynamic, one also comes to a better understanding of how individual attitudes are ultimately linked to the productivity of business firms.

It is no wonder that the link between individual job satisfaction and productivity has been hard to establish. The framework developed here suggests that an individual's satisfaction with work is influenced by satisfaction with the various agents that will represent her/his interests. These relationships are complicated and constantly changing. Nevertheless, psychological theory has helped to understand the dynamics and has served as a useful complement to the economic, political, and sociological theories presented in earlier chapters.

Summary

Achieving an acceptable transaction between an individual and an organization is often problematic, and one of the important problems is the degree of control exercised by the organization over an individual's behavior. From psychologists one learns that control per se is not necessarily good or bad. Societal controls are ubiquitous—one is surrounded by countless controls over behavior. What is important is the nature of controls—whether aversive or not—and who is to be entrusted with changing their shape.

In this chapter I have presented a theoretical framework in which to understand the negotiation over new or changed controls, and I have described what the changes in controls will imply for individuals and their bargaining agents. Negotiations occur over which of several centers of control will predominate, if any. But in no sense is it assumed that individuals or their bargaining representatives will be able to escape entirely the control of the market, the control of the firm, the control of the government, or the control of the union. Individuals seek solutions to labor problems by balancing controls—thereby seeking to protect individual autonomy, avoid alienating work, and guarantee a minimum level of job security.

In this chapter, I have also discussed the psychological underpinnings of economic and social behavior. Kaufman's (1989) contention that all industrial relations research be based on an underlying model of human psychology was examined. The conflict analyzed by sociologists often stems from feelings of alienation, inequity, or injustice. The negotiation analyzed by institutionalist economists often originates in an individual's fear that jobs are scarce and need to be protected. The decision to quit or take a job described by neoclassical economists is often affected by a person's sense of loyalty to the firm's objectives. In all these cases, psychologists have provided the individual groundwork over which institutional theory is constructed.

Chapter 7

INDUSTRIAL RELATIONS AND
THE SOCIAL SCIENCES: THE LONG VIEW

Organizations in which industrial relations must be understood are becoming increasingly complex. On the one hand, these organizations have become more differentiated—firms are now more decentralized. Increasingly, firms seek to maximize individual potential, empower individual employees, and give workers more choice about the rewards gained from work (cafeteria benefit plans, work tailored to individual demands, and greater flexibility in work hours, for example). Yet the operations of such firms also require a high degree of integration. Just-in-time inventory systems, total quality management, and sophisticated information systems put considerable pressure on employees to coordinate their functions with others. The increased demands on employees to work together in teams requires commitment to the firm's overall goals.

In point of fact, both differentiation and integration can be seen as integral to a definition of organizational complexity:

Differentiation refers to the degree to which a system (i.e., an organ such as the brain, or an individual, a family, a corporation, a culture, or humanity as a whole) is composed of parts that differ in structure or function from one another. *Integration* refers to the extent to which the different parts communicate and enhance one another's goals. A system that is more differentiated and integrated than another is said to be more *complex.* (Csikszentmihalyi 1993, 156)

Seen within this book's framework, industrial relations explains how negotiation of issues that span various centers of control occur as markets, business organizations, government, and other agents that represent workers become increasingly complex. Individuals who engage in these negotiations are performing at the organizational level the very thing people seek to do at a personal level:

A person is differentiated to the extent that he or she has many different interests, abilities, and goals: he or she is integrated in proportion to the

131

harmony that exists between various goals and between thought, feel-ings, and action. A person who is only differentiated might be a genius but is likely to suffer from inner conflicts. One who is only integrated might experience inner peace, but is not likely to make a contribution to culture. . . . Complexity, at any level of analysis, involves the optimal development of both differentiation and integration. (Csikszentmihalyi 1993, 156–57)

Negotiations in industrial relations can be thought of as the process of bring-ing together different interests, abilities, and goals to achieve—if not total har-mony—at least a certain kind of coordinated work effort.

One can hardly help notice the number of references to harmony (or lack thereof) that have occurred throughout this review of social science theory. The classical economist assumed a minimal degree of harmony for the functioning of competitive markets. Institutional economists who were in dissent argued that harmony would have to be created and that the process would not be easy—in fact, it would be a process ridden with conflict and the need for sophisticated methods to resolve conflict. Sociologists trained in systems theory substituted the term stability for harmony as they analyzed how social systems resist change. Sociologists assumed that except in periods of extraordinary change, systems would have self-adjusting mechanisms that would maintain the system over time. Others of a more radical bent saw the lack of harmony between social classes as the major problem confronting workers and revolutionary change as the expected outcome. For political scientists, harmonizing differing value sys-tems was the aim of political activity, and for psychologists, harmony was re-lated to the integration of personality and feelings of satisfaction, equity, and justice.

Though a greater degree of harmony might be hoped for, conflict is often the reality—conflicting goals within organizations, conflicting values, conflict among classes and other groups within society and conflict among individuals. Conflict may also occur between an individual and the organization that is to serve as the individual's agent. A dynamic of trust and distrust may lead indi-viduals to shift from one agent to another in an effort to avoid the exploitation and/or job insecurity that comes from too much control centered in the market, the firm, the labor union or government. I now turn once again to look at spe-cific workplace issues and to see how this review helps in understanding the negotiations that occur as industrial relations systems become increasingly com-plex. Described below are each of the human resource activities from the original framework presented in chapter 1 (figures 1.2–1.5). Summaries of the predic-tions developed in subsequent chapters are applied to each of the separate hu-man resource activities.

Negotiational Issues Involved in the Development of Human Resources

Figure 1.2's depiction of development activities describes the variety of ways in which training can be provided. The figure also shows the conflict an individual might feel when considering the benefits and costs of each process. The processes located at the extremes of figure 1.2 are shown at numbers one, five, nine, and eleven. At the market extreme, the business firm or private for-profit education and training institutions provide all the training an individual will receive. The system is efficient since only those skills that are demanded for employment will be provided. One might have been willing to grant such a system at least some degree of trust had not Karl Marx, through his writing, raised this implicit question: what if the private system for training is controlled by a class of people whose interests are diametrically opposed to those who are to be trained? Instead of being trained, employees could become de-skilled. Automation, division of labor, and ever-increasing unemployment would force workers' into a precarious existence and into severe conflict with those providing the training. The result would be either revolt or a search for new agents to represent employee interests in the area of training and development.

Labor unions and government alike could serve employee interests, but at the extremes, they too would be in a position to exploit their power. At number one, government provides all training services. According to political scientists, conflicting societal values would then come into play. Government would decide who should receive training. But those supporting political authorities (those with connections) might be first in the queue. Consciously formulated government policy might direct training on the basis of needs, but how would it be decided who is most needy? At number eleven, training is provided through a tightly controlled, craft union apprenticeship system with all the potential for discrimination that such a system entails. Sons and daughters and close acquaintances of craftsworkers would be first to gain admission.

Based on this review, I predict that no one center of control should totally prevail in the negotiation that occurs over how training services will be provided. Political negotiation will undoubtedly enable government to provide some form of subsidized training—either through a public education system or through special government-funded training programs. Other training will be undertaken by private firms. Economic theory predicts that private firms would have an incentive to provide only the kind of training that is not transferable to other firms. Nevertheless, through negotiation, one would expect employees to obtain some general training as well. Employees will try to obtain benefits like tuition reimbursement from their employers to limit the firm's power over human resource development. General training increases the individual's power by increasing their ability to quit and take their training elsewhere.

This book's review of sociological literature indicates that negotiation over training will vary in difficulty depending on the strength of the class structure. If decisions about skill development are left to the owners of capital and if, as a class, these owners control government as well as private firms, then it would be hard for government to serve as an agent for employees. When neither government nor the business firm serves as an agent for an individual's human resource development, workers may turn to collective means for controlling skill acquisition (craft unions) or insist that market forces be strengthened to allow individuals more leeway in providing their own training (students loans, for example).

A sociological perspective also shows that the development of human resources should be thought of in terms broader than the workplace. Neoclassical economists argued that a country's economic growth would be enhanced by efficient, competitive markets, but these economists assumed a certain degree of social harmony that would permit this to happen. Institutional economists argued that difficult negotiation over the rules of human resource development would require carefully constructed institutions other than the market—public training institutions, an educational system, scholarships, and student loans. Marxists differed sharply from either neoclassical or institutional economists by assuming that the path of economic development over time would lead to increased class conflict, decreased skill and autonomy for workers, and ultimately, dramatic changes in the entire system. Though today, free-market and institutionalist views seem to prevail over Marxist views, the debate among these widely differing perspectives has not been fully resolved.

Negotiational Issues Involved in the Allocation of Human Resources

Allocational processes located at the extreme centers of control in figure 1.3 are numbers one, six, eleven, and fifteen. These are processes that have the highest potential for exploitation and the largest risk of job insecurity. At number six, individuals are subject to an unregulated, competitive market and would therefore be under the greatest pressure to adjust quickly to changes in demand and/or technology. Under such circumstances, the system is highly differentiated since individuals and firms are free to pursue their own interests. The market is expected to perform an integrating function and achieve harmony by matching people efficiently to firms where their skills will be most useful. The high degree of competition and the potential requirement for rapid change make it difficult to achieve harmony within such a system unless all those in the system have values that mesh extraordinarily well. If not, one expects individuals to seek out or create for themselves agents to represent their interests in a negotiated settlement.

The boundaries for negotiation can be seen in figure 1.3. If control is centered wholly in government, the firm, or the labor union, government-controlled job placement, slavery, and hiring halls will be the respective outcomes. In each case, the potential for exploitation is high—especially if the agents are not democratically controlled. Negotiated settlements are expected to occur with regard to affirmative action, comparable worth, job posting systems, human resource planning, and union shop arrangements. Negotiations will occur among the various agents with each claiming to represent the interests of employees. Reference will be made to the free-market alternative as a basis for comparison, but in the end, negotiations will produce a reasonable settlement. Benchmarks will likely be based on the customary practices of the best firms. Some form of government control over hiring and firing practices will undoubtedly be established—coupled with a number of internal regulations over posting of jobs and transfers that will be established by large firms.

Labor unions are expected to be involved as agents for individual employees by bargaining for economic benefits, grievance procedures, and work rules. Unions, pseudo unions, and fairly extensive grievance procedures are expected to be strongest in firms where the market causes a high degree of insecurity. In such a case, employees will lose faith in the market and turn to the union as an agent for protection. Unions will also be strong when they are democratically governed, when trust in their agency function is high, and when political values are such that unions are seen to be a democratizing force in industry and in the society at large. Unions will be strong when members believe they need protection from exploitation by other groups or classes within society. Unions may also occur in firms that have agency problems with their employees; however, an employer is more likely to choose other ways of granting employees a voice in the firm's decision making. This type of employee influence is most likely in those cases where the expectations that a firm has for its employees cannot readily be written down in a formal contract and where employees have considerable autonomy, a high degree of firm specific skill, and responsibility that, if misused, could cost the firm dearly. A good example is a service firm with decentralized operations whose skilled employees must project a good image for the company and make quick decisions in response to consumer demands.

Negotiational Issues Involved in the Utilization of Human Resources

The extremes in control over human resource utilization are shown at numbers one, five, eleven, and fourteen of figure 1.4. At number five, societal decisions about variation in the way labor and capital are to be combined are left entirely to private firms. The economic system is left uncontrolled and assumed to be able to correct itself when periods of unemployment or inflation occur. At another extreme (number one), government authority determines the rate of investment, how many people will be hired by each firm, and how much individuals will be paid. At number eleven, private firms dictate wages and working conditions, to some degree independent of market forces, and at number fourteen, unions protect past arrangements for work rules even after technological change and/or market forces make them outmoded. Virtually all of the social sciences have contributed to the dynamics of how an industrial relations system would reach or resist these extremes, but their analysis has been very different from one discipline to another.

Psychologists, through their discussion of control mechanisms, have provided perhaps the most important theoretical framework for understanding human resource utilization. Human relations scholars became known for their insistence that control over the work environment was not as important as understanding the human side of the enterprise. Yet this unwillingness to focus on who is at the controls irritated labor leaders and led many to conclude that human relations was but one part of an ill-advised bag of management tricks to be relied upon to manipulate the workforce. Today, the same skepticism has been transferred to the practice of human resource management.

At another extreme was Karl Marx who did not hesitate for a minute to name who was in charge—the capitalist. Marx used the more value laden term exploitation, instead of utilization, when he analyzed workplace activity.[1] According to Marx, a portion of the value of workplace activity that rightfully belonged to the workforce was expropriated by the capitalist. Who was in control definitely mattered in Marx's analysis of class relationships.

Somewhere between these two extremes was the thinking of William Foote Whyte who argued that Mayo and his followers misinterpreted their own experiments and, in the process, set back research on autonomous work groups for many years. Ultimately, such autonomous groups would be negotiated as shown by the activities that lie at midpoints between extreme centers of control in figure 1.4—autonomous work groups, teamwork, joint labor-management committees, quality circles, and works councils. I contend that, through negotiation, industrial relations systems will avoid the extremes in human resource utilization shown in figure 1.4, and institutions of shared control will increasingly be adopted.

Psychologists and students of human resource management might object to this facile prediction of shared control—particularly with regard to such managerial prerogatives as compensation and other workplace factors that can be manipulated to produce work effort. A review of sociological literature, however, revealed a widespread belief that basic social processes of negotiation are hard to ignore, even in those areas considered to be managerial rights. Granovetter and Tilly (1988), in particular, associate the variation in pay rates that exist in industrial economies not with competitiveness in labor markets, but rather with bargaining power and unequal access to a complex web of interpersonal networks in society. In their opinion, variation in wage rates is not so much a function of competition, rationalized job descriptions, and performance appraisal as it is a strongly sociological process of comparisons made within firms and in the local community.

The workplace activities shown in figure 1.4 only indirectly show another aspect of the utilization of human resources—namely the individual sentiments that occur as different human resource management practices are put in place. An indirect manifestation of such feelings is the grievance process where employees can give voice to their feelings. Grievance procedures are shown at the midpoint between two centers of control—the market and the firm, reflecting the belief that control concentrated wholly in the market or in the firm would not permit the airing and resolution of feelings like alienation, inequity, or injustice. Where control is concentrated at either extreme, employees would have to leave or threaten to leave jobs just to have their grievances addressed. Along with Hirschman (1970), I argue that most employees would prefer to negotiate for grievance procedures and remain loyal to their firms rather than exit. When the costs of training and keeping employees is high, an employer should likewise protect her/his interests by maintaining employee loyalty.

Industrial relations, through its analysis of grievance institutions, deals with the socio-psychological side of organizational life. At the extremes of human resource utilization activities, other social science disciplines come into play. Economists have created a logical and consistent explanation for how choices are made when exit to the market, rather than negotiation, alters the match between specific job responsibilities and individual abilities and skills. The human relations and Marxist schools of thought apply when power is concentrated in the firm's management. Institutionalist economists and political scientists who view the firm as a form of government have much to say about the negotiations that occur when human resource utilization policies are codified into the firm's operational manual.

Negotiational Issues Involved in the Maintenance
of Human Resources

At one time, institutionalist economists would be the primary group identified with the maintenance of human resources. The maintenance function after the Great Depression was seen to be primarily a government responsibility. Unemployment insurance, worker's compensation, social security insurance, and disability insurance were developed, in the United States at least, through government legislation and with the help of institutionalists who made recommendations for the types of rules that should govern these important innovations. A look at figure 1.5, however, shows that today the picture is more complex. Unions administer health and pension plans. Companies provide employee assistance programs and negotiate health care plans for their employees.

As in the case of other human resource functions, maintenance can have big drawbacks for individuals if provided at the extreme positions of control shown in figure 1.5. At the market extreme, individuals would be expected to carry a great deal of insurance and have considerable foresight regarding the social risks that are possible over a lifetime of work. These individuals would have to protect against the loss of income that occurs at retirement and have to carry unemployment, disability, health, and injury insurance from private companies. More importantly, individuals would have to prove that any hazards that befell them were not of their own doing. Courts would be filled with litigation between individuals and their insurers. The uncertainty and complexity of such a system would undoubtedly leave many uninsured, underinsured, worried, or confused.

At union- and firm-level extremes, power over the type of insurance coverage provided is left in the hands of a few people who may not be accountable to those who are insured. Unions that are not well controlled democratically and operate pension plans for their members may be tempted to borrow from reserves. Employers may try to cut costs by purchasing pension plans that are underfunded—giving the impression that they are providing maintenance protection that is safe when in reality it is not. If government provides all social insurance, an impersonal bureaucracy that responds poorly to changing conditions or to individual circumstances may be the result.

As a consequence of the above disadvantages, I predict a negotiated solution to the problems of human resource maintenance. Private insurance will be supplemented by government- and firm-provided insurance plans, but negotiation will seek to avoid the extremes shown in figure 1.5. Institutionalist thinking helps in understanding the types of negotiations that will occur. Many of these negotiations will be fought out through the courts. Broad definitions written into public law will be interpreted in court to devise workable definitions of the circumstances under which various forms of insurance will be called upon to protect individuals. If, however, the courts are relied on exclusively to provide such guidance, the outcome may not be acceptable to the parties who negotiated the maintenance protection in the first place. Institutionalists argue that joint committees should be established to work out the ongoing problems of interpretation. The hearings process in worker's compensation is a good example. Through this process issues like whether a person is able to return to work or whether light work should be required are decided before a hearing officer—but outside the court system. The solutions to problems regarding maintenance are not neatly determined. In many cases, all parties must agree to a solution that is reasonable.

The Dynamics of the Workplace

The diagrams as drawn in figures 1.2–1.5 place the market center of control at the top. Does this imply that the market-oriented location is preferred because it is uppermost in the diagram? Are there historical forces akin to gravitational forces that drive activities downward from the market position and toward more control by the firm, by the union, or by government? Are institutions necessary to forestall movement toward one or another center of control?

By positioning the market center of control at the top of the diagram shown in figure 1.1, an assumption is not being made that, over time, control will gravitate from the market to the other centers in the lower part of the diagram. What is implied is that the market can serve as a single alternative to all of the other potential centers of control. One should assume no automatic tendency for control to revert to any one center of control, however.

The dynamics proposed here are as follows: markets, though desired for their efficiency in allocation of resources and their contribution to economic growth, create a high degree of uncertainty for individuals—especially during historical periods of rapid economic change. Individuals will continuously seek to protect themselves from the insecurity of markets through their agents, but at some point the desire for additional individual freedom and choice will prevent control from being concentrated too heavily in one or another of the protective institutions used to shield individuals from the market. The system's dynamics will move it back toward more market control or toward another agent that will have countervailing power. The creation of new protective agents will be most likely during historical periods of rapid economic change.

To test the utility of the model thus developed, I have examined several instances in which the dynamics of the industrial relations system were important: (1) the time period during which factory production displaced agrarian production for the first time, namely during the European industrial revolution; (2) the industrial age—a time period after which a number of countries industrialized and during which some industrial relations scholars expected industrial relations institutions to become more and more similar—to converge; and (3) the time period during which a number of third-world countries sought to accelerate their own economic development after key countries had already achieved rapid growth based on industrialization.

The Industrial Revolution

Interpretation of the industrial revolution is very different depending on the assumptions one makes about the dynamics of economic development and the centers of control that were most important over time. One alternative is to assume that control during the industrial revolution was located primarily in the market. If this was true, then new, high-paying jobs in urban factories would have been the main factor in attracting labor from the countryside as industrialization occurred. Individual labor market choices would have expanded as rural workers discovered the new jobs, responded to economic signals (urban wage rates), and moved to urban areas. The opening up of new employment opportunities coupled with a higher rate of economic growth for the country would have increased the well-being of everyone—despite potential conflict over the distribution of the benefits throughout society. Labor unions, from this viewpoint, were at best instruments for securing a more equitable distribution of the benefits derived from growth; at worst, unions were a hindrance to sustained growth.

A quite different view of the industrial revolution results if one assumes that control within the economic system rested originally with firms (in this case agricultural landowners). In Britain prior to the industrial revolution, the nobility owned (and thereby, controlled) large tracts of agricultural land. Some of the land was enclosed, but some was left unenclosed for the common pasturing rights of tenant farmers. In the early nineteenth century, more and more of the land was enclosed, thereby forcing peasant farmers to leave rural areas and join the growing urban working class. These individuals were not drawn to new factory jobs by way of market forces (according to this historical interpretation), but were pushed to factory employment due to the exercise of control over agricultural land by British landowners. Once in factory employment, the new urban workforce found itself under the control of the factory owners. Resentment led to a strong demand for agents to help workers regain the sense of control they had lost in the move from agriculture to the urban factory system. The agency function for workers was fulfilled by the British government which regulated and slowed the process of enclosure through legislation passed in the mid-nineteenth century. In part, the agency function was fulfilled through labor unions who ultimately negotiated with factory owners over the rules of employment. Control was shifted from one centered largely on the landed nobility and factory owners to control shared among government, landowners, factory owners, trade unions, and the market.

The dynamics of control described above have produced two competing hypotheses to account for the development of unions after the industrial revolution. An examination of the specific activities implied by these two competing hypotheses should help in deciding which is more consistent with historical fact. One type of human resource activity was critical: maintenance. Peasant farmers who were maintained on the land due to common grazing acreage left to take factory work. Why were they maintained on the land originally? Did large landowners not want to maintain them on the land and purposefully remove their livelihoods through enclosure? What were the reactions of the peasants—resentment toward the landowners or satisfaction regarding the greater degree of choice afforded to them by urban employment? Answers to these questions are difficult, but historical analysis appears to support the notion that an important protective agent was removed involuntarily from peasants. As a result, the peasants were forced to rely on the market for their livelihood which caused an unacceptable degree of uncertainty. In reaction, workers would ultimately create a new protective mechanism for themselves—the labor union (Polanyi 1957; Tannenbaum 1952).

Industrial Relations Dynamics in the Industrial Age

A number of industrial relations scholars have predicted that labor unions would behave similarly from country to country as industrial technology made their negotiating relationships with government and private firms more and more alike (Ross and Hartman 1960; Kerr et al. 1960). After undertaking an ambitious study of economic development in a number of countries, Kerr and his colleagues were deeply impressed by the effects of industrial technology on all other aspects of social life. They argued that despite initial cultural differences, the homogenizing effects of industrial technology would be strong enough to cause convergence of different industrial relations systems. Labor unions, government, and industry would ultimately relate to each other in similar ways from one industrialized country to another. But how have individuals sought out agents to protect their interests in the thirty years since these predictions were made? Does the search for agents indicate convergence?

The proportion of the labor movement that is unionized within a country is perhaps the simplest dimension on which to test for convergence, and here the evidence is not good. In the last twenty years, the labor movement has lost influence in some countries (United States, Great Britain), while in others (Canada, Poland, Korea) it has either maintained or rapidly gained influence. On a second dimension—the nature of bargaining between unions and employers—there is likewise little evidence of convergence. Japan maintains a system of enterprise unions that covers about one-fourth of the workforce. Bargaining is done once a year with coordination provided by the national union federation. Swedish labor unions continue to bargain wages nationally with an employer's association for virtually all employees in the country, as they have since the early part of this century. Germany combines industrywide collective bargaining with a system of works councils and codetermination that other countries have not emulated. The United States bargains almost exclusively at the plant level, as it has since the National Labor Relations Act was passed in the 1930s.

These two dimensions alone (percent unionized and bargaining structure) show that even if industrial technology has had a strong homogenizing effect, it must have been counteracted by other forces preventing convergence. Those other forces could well be related to strong underlying societal preferences for the degree of control granted to management, government, labor unions, and the market. Evidently, industrial technology has, at least until now, been sufficiently adaptable to permit countries to follow different strategies of shared control and still provide their citizens with an acceptable rate of economic growth.

Convergence may have been defined too narrowly, however. In the framework of this book, countries do not have to negotiate with precisely the same institutions in order to converge. Given the significant differences in cultural values that underlie the process, countries would not likely negotiate as such. What one should look for is whether there is a general tendency in every country to avoid the extreme centers of control shown in the figures above. Convergence, according to this definition, means that countries design industrial relations systems around institutions shown at the midpoints of figures 1.2–1.5. And here, convergence seems to occur in a very rough sense. Over time, the extremes do seem to be avoided. Labor movements do continue to appear in countries that have relied heavily on total government control or total market control over the employment relationship. Negotiated solutions to the problems of human resource development, allocation, utilization, and maintenance result in a variety of changing institutional arrangements, but they all have in common the objective to avoid too high a degree of control in any one of the centers shown in figures 1.2–1.5.

Industrial Relations Dynamics and
Third-world Economic Development

An important problem in industrial society is the personal insecurity associated with freely functioning, competitive markets. In the context of third-world economic development, economic insecurity is often associated with inadequate or unstable employment. Yet insecurity can also be associated with income inequality. Richer nations may invest in the natural resource industries of poorer nations, thereby creating industrial enclaves where stable employment exists for a small number of highly paid workers (oil, for example). But if profits are not spread to other sectors of the developing country's economy, employment elsewhere may remain highly insecure and unstable. Despite any economic growth that occurs in the two sectors combined, the dualism in development may leave the labor problem unresolved for large numbers of people.[2] Within a specific country as well, a high degree of inequality of income can affect the labor problem significantly. Unequal incomes may occur under a system of property ownership where a few wealthy landowners have high economic security while large numbers of tenants live in an equally insecure situation engaged in subsistence farming. In either of the above two cases, a collective response to the labor problem can lead to a more regulated market economy—nationalization of the country's natural resource firms or a policy of import substitution in the first instance and land reform in the second. Through political channels, the developing country's industrial unions may lobby hard for nationalization and import substitution whereas farmer's unions may strongly support land reform.

A negotiated choice made by a country regarding its development path is a relatively new idea in economic development thought. Negotiated choices imply that more than one set of technologies could be relied upon to provide equally satisfactory growth. A single set of technical conditions may not be the only prerequisite for growth as implied in Rostow's book, *The Stages of Economic Growth* (1960), or in other early theories of development. In addition, a country may not have to incur a high degree of income inequality to achieve growth, as argued by Kuznets.[3] Increasingly, development economists argue that the expected degree of future income inequality, not just growth in national income, should help shape overall development strategy (Chenery and Srinivasan 1988, chap. 19).

The concept of choice in economic development strategy has led some theorists to ask whether the existence of already developed, industrialized countries in the world has restricted the choices available to others. Dependency theorists, for example, argue that the world's system of trade has confined less developed economies to the periphery of the world economy. The rules of trade are negotiated by the more developed countries to create initial benefits for the economies at the center, with additional benefits gradually spreading out to economies at the periphery (Prebisch 1959).

Dependency theory, coupled with dissatisfaction over the slow rate at which benefits spread from the center to the periphery, have resulted in a demand for change in the international rules of trade. The United Nations declaration of May 1974, for example, called for a New International Economic Order (NIEO)—"a reconstruction of the existing international economic system to improve the development prospects for developing countries, [thereby] narrowing [the] disparities between rich and poor countries . . . and giving them more control over the shape of their development goals and strategies" (Chenery and Srinivasan 1988, 1290). Because reconstruction of the world economic system involves bargaining between rich and poor countries, the NIEO proposal is an important part of the negotiation over paths for economic development—but in this case an international rather than a domestic negotiation.[4] Such negotiation could have a strong relationship with how a specific country deals with what has been called the labor problem.

To date, theories of industrial relations and economic development have not overlapped much—with the notable exception of the theory of convergence already discussed above. A view of economic development based on negotiated choice rather than technological determinism provides more room for joining the two areas. The framework developed in this book suggests several ways in which the two are related. To some degree the labor problem as defined here is also the problem of economic development—to provide an adequate degree of economic growth and an adequate degree of economic security. But to these two goals, economic development strategists, particularly those advocating a new international economic order, would add a third: an adequate degree of income equality. How does this definition of the labor problem fit with the overall framework of analysis developed here?

A redefinition of the labor problem to include the degree of income equality fits uncomfortably into the framework developed in this book. The issue of how income should be distributed is allocation, but not the allocation of human resources—rather the allocation of material resources. By locating the labor problem in the workplace of an individual firm, my model ignores the distribution of income. But should it? Is the distribution of income generated by the market always legitimate (however the labor problem is to be resolved in the workplace)? Is resolution of the labor problem unaffected by individual perceptions of fairness regarding the distribution of income? Negative answers to the above questions must lead to a modification of the original framework. The labor problem may need to be resolved not only in the workplace but also in the public arena where tax rate changes and other policies of income distribution can be debated. What began as an economic problem involving workplace issues has, in part, become a problem of political economy involving national tax and spending policies.

Other aspects of the labor problem, as seen in economic development, fit well into this book's theoretical framework. For example, the twin problems of utilization and allocation of human resources have been a preoccupation of development economists for many years. Initially, Lewis argued that the traditional sector of the economy would provide unlimited supplies of labor to the modern sector as economic development proceeded. Only when large numbers of underemployed rural workers were absorbed by the modern sector would wages begin to rise in the traditional sector—making mechanization of agriculture profitable. Perverse results could occur if capital intensive industries dominated the modern sector while excessive population growth occurred in the rural sector—agriculture could become more and more labor intensive and less productive as overall economic growth continued. The potential role of agrarian or industrial unions in negotiating more favorable outcomes was ignored because the use of efficient, but capital intensive, technology in the modern sector of the economy was viewed as unavoidable. The system had to accommodate the limited growth in employment that could be expected from the modern sector.

The views of Lewis and others who argue that inflexible technology could seriously constrain the path of economic development have recently been challenged. Inadequate financing of the type of technology that creates jobs (financial dualism) may have constrained the growth in good jobs, not imported technology itself (Meier 1984, 173). Government policy encouraging adequate financing of employment-creating investment does not occur automatically, however—some form of political or economic negotiation must precede the policy. A politicized labor movement in coalition with groups representing the interests of small- and medium-sized firms could be critical forces in preventing financial dualism.

Using the framework developed in this book and combining it with economic development theory yields a picture of two quite undesirable solutions to the labor problem. First, a move toward unregulated financing of economic development by private firms, especially through foreign investment, may result in an undesirable allocation of labor between the modern and traditional sectors of the economy. Imported capital intensive technology, by definition, does not utilize much labor and often creates a small high-wage enclave in the midst of an economy that may also be characterized by high unemployment. Secondly, a move to heavy government control in all markets (including the labor market) may be equally undesirable, even if it occurs as a reaction to the private sector solution. Government may subsidize industries that have a higher degree of employment-creating potential than those created in the modern sector through private investment alone. High tariff barriers may be built around infant industries with the promise of future reductions once industries have grown up (which they often never do). Government may provide employment by investing in a variety of industries itself or by expanding government services quite rapidly—arguing that resolution of its labor problems requires adequate maintenance—such as unemployment insurance, health insurance, public pensions, and a variety of other services associated with the modern welfare state. The absence of competition in providing these services and the government's resulting tendency to employ excessive numbers of people can result in serious inefficiency, inflation, and stagnation in overall economic growth.

The industrial relations framework developed here argues for an economic development policy that avoids unregulated private sector control or a high degree of government control. Countries that most successfully avoid either extreme will be those that build institutions to serve as agents for employees and persons likely to invest in employment-creating projects—often the owners of small- and medium-sized firms. Once organized, agricultural unions, associations of cattle producers, associations of small businesses, federations of cooperatives, and industrial unions will need a forum in which to debate and negotiate over alternative plans for economic development. Because labor unions are expected to be active in negotiations over a country's development path, one final implication can be drawn. Labor unions in third-world countries will undoubtedly be highly political—concerned with economic security, but also with a route toward economic development and the distribution of income.

The presumption that the labor problem and the problem of economic development are interrelated has led to a new application of the framework developed in this book. In the process, the framework has been expanded. No longer is the labor problem defined to apply to the workplace alone. Instead, the societal issue of income distribution is also addressed. The framework has allowed one to envision problems associated with a variety of economic development paths. The less complicated world of economic development based on adjustment to the dictates of new technology becomes a more complicated, negotiated world of choice among various competing technologies—each with its own set of outcomes.

Summary

From the workplace of a single industrial firm to an entire country's process of economic development planning, social science theory has helped address the problem of work in an industrial society. The problem is multidimensional, and a single social science discipline often addresses only one or two aspects at a time. Thus, industrial relations scholars need to debate the merits of alternative theories, integrate theories that complement each other, and draw new insights from the combined perspectives these theories help to create. Partial theories tested in the workplace are coupled with long-term, historical analysis to obtain predictions about the dynamics of industrial relationships over time. Much is undetermined and merely a function of the strategies and power of the actors in the industrial relations system, but the direction taken by negotiation is clear. Powerful centers of control will be avoided. Negotiation will seek to establish a variety of institutions from which individual employees can choose to represent their interests over time. At times, the system may move strongly in the direction of control that is concentrated in government, the firm, the market, or the union, but eventually new collective agents will be created thereby preventing total concentration of control in any one center.

Notes

Chapter 1:
Social Sciences and the Employment Relationship

1. The same point was made earlier by Somers (1968).

2. The activities are merely illustrative and definitely do not include all activities that could be envisioned under each subheading of the employment relationship.

3. This, of course, is only one of the reasons for compulsory education financed by government.

4. This is despite the fact that Private Employment Councils in the United States typically involve informal negotiating among groups that may differ in their interests regarding training.

Chapter 2:
Origins of the Field of Industrial Relations

1. The reaction in the United States was to the overall political system of Communism. McCarthyism should certainly not be denied. American institutionalists were very much involved in politics since Commons and his students were very active in building American institutions of social security, largely through the Democratic Party. But they were not ideological in the sense of building a political movement that would run counter to Marxist ideology.

Chapter 4:
Social Systems, Conflict, and Change

1. Notice that the social solidarity of strikers among themselves may create community obligations for mutual support similar to those provided by the tribe in premarket societies. Social solidarity may therefore substitute, in part, for a lack of support from the broader community.

Chapter 5:
Neo-institutionalists, Economics, and Industrial Relations

1. Hsieh and Mangum support their assertion by reference to a review of classical writers (Smith, Ricardo, Bentham, J. S. Mill, and others) by Samuels (1966).

2. See, for example, Barbash 1989.

3. For additional information on agency theory, see Jensen 1983, Jensen and Meckling 1976, and Mirrlees 1976.

4. Williamson defines opportunism as acting in one's own self-interest with guile (1985, 30).

Chapter 6:
The Psychologists and Industrial Relations

1. German psychologist Hugo Munsterberg (1913) believed that psychology could be applied to the humanization of jobs.

2. Barbash (1991, 349) puts it as follows: "Business unionism lives in a world of limits which spring from fear of cooptation by management and from fear of spreading itself too thinly." Then he lists a number of limits (or controls) under which the union must work: collective bargaining must be employment centered; key decisions must be made by the rank and file; "grieving" against the company fits better with the union's mission than partnership with management; the strike is a means to a better agreement, not an end in itself; and unions may disagree with each other, making it necessary to have clear jurisdictions.

3. Scientific management is one of the earliest examples (Taylor 1911, 197).

4. The research was carried out at Western Electric where banks of wires were connected, hence "bank wiring room."

5. See, for example, the excellent chapter on scientific management in Bendix 1956.

6. See Eilbert 1959 or Nelson 1975 for two accounts of the historical development of personnel management in the United States.

7. Marriott Hotels was the first to introduce a centralized computer reservation system. This enabled the hotel chain to take advantage of greater worker initiative and economies of scale (Kaestle 1990).

Chapter 7:
Industrial Relations and the Social Sciences: The Long View

1. The term *utilization* is hardly value free, however, because it implies that one person is using another—a form of exploitation.

2. See Meier 1984, 149–214, for a detailed discussion of dualism in economic development theory.

3. After examining a cross section of countries at different stages of development, Kuznets (1955) observed that the distribution of income over time would assume the shape of an inverted U as industrialization occurred, starting with a fairly equal distribution, becoming highly unequal, and then returning to a position of greater equality.

4. Despite its importance, the NIEO has not led to significant changes in the system of international trade. Reasons for its failure are discussed in chap. 24 of Chenery and Srinivasan 1988, 1290–92.

BIBLIOGRAPHY

Adams, J. S. 1965. "Inequity in Social Exchange." *Advances in Experimental Social Psychology* 2:267–99.

Adams, Roy. 1988a. "Desperately Seeking Industrial Relations Theory." *The International Journal of Comparative Labour, Law and Industrial Relations* 4, no. 1:1–10.

Adams, Roy. 1988b. "The Role of Management in a Political Conception of the Employment Relationship." In *Management Under Differing Labour Market and Employment Systems,* edited by G. Dlugos, W. Dorow, and K. Weiermair. Berlin: de Gruyter.

Adams, Roy, and Noah Meltz. 1993. *Industrial Relations Theory: Its Nature, Scope, and Pedagogy.* Metuchen, N.J. and London: Scarecrow Press.

Aitken, Hugh. 1960. *Taylorism at Waterton Arsenal: Scientific Management in Action.* Cambridge, Mass.: Harvard University Press.

Bakke, E. Wight. 1969. *The Mission of Manpower Policy.* Kalamazoo, Mich.: Upjohn Institute.

Ballou, Dale, and Michael Podgursky. 1993. "Teachers' Attitudes Toward Merit Pay: Examining Conventional Wisdom." *Industrial and Labor Relations Review* 47 (October): 50–61.

Bandura, A. 1977. *Social Learning Theory.* Englewood Cliffs, N.J.: Prentice-Hall.

Barbash, Jack. 1967. "John R. Commons and the Americanization of the Labor Problem." *Journal of Economic Issues* 1 (September): 161–67.

Barbash, Jack. 1984. *The Elements of Industrial Relations.* Madison: University of Wisconsin Press.

Barbash, Jack. 1989. "John R. Commons: Pioneer of Labor Economics." *Monthly Labor Review* 112 (May): 44–49.

Barbash, Jack. 1991. "American Trade Unionism: The State of the Art." In *The State of the Unions,* edited by G. Strauss et al. Madison, Wis.: Industrial Relations Research Association.

Becker, G. 1962. "Investment in Human Capital: A Theoretical Analysis." *Journal of Political Economy* 70, supplement (October): 9–44.

Becker, Gary. 1975. *Human Capital.* 2d ed. New York: Columbia University Press.

Begin, James. 1991. *Strategic Employment Policy: An Organization Systems Perspective.* Englewood Cliffs, N.J.: Prentice-Hall.

Bell, Daniel. 1973. *The Coming of Post-Industrial Society.* New York: Basic Books.

Bendix, R., and R. H. Fisher. 1961. "The Perspectives of Elton Mayo." In *Complex Organizations: A Sociological Reader,* edited by A. Etzioni. New York: Holt, Rinehart, and Winston.

Bendix, Reinhard. 1956. *Work and Authority in Industry.* New York: Wiley.

Blumer, Herbert. 1969. *Symbolic Interactionism: Perspective and Method.* Englewood Cliffs, N.J.: Prentice-Hall.

Brauer, David. 1990. "Does Centralized Collective Bargaining Promote Wage Restraint? The Case of Israel." *Industrial and Labor Relations Review* 43 (July): 636–49.

Braverman, Harry. 1974. *Labor and Monopoly Capital: The Degradation of Work in the 20th Century.* New York: Monthly Review Press.

Burack, E., and J. Walker, eds. 1972. *Manpower Planning and Programming.* Boston: Allyn and Bacon.

Burawoy, Michael. 1978. "Toward a Marxist Theory of the Labor Process: Braverman and Beyond." *Politics and Society* 8:247–312.

Burawoy, Michael. 1979. *Manufacturing Consent: Change in the Labor Process Under Monopoly Capitalism.* Chicago: University of Chicago Press.

Cain, Glen G., and Robinson G. Hollister. 1969. "The Methodology of Evaluating Social Action Programs." In *Public-Private Manpower Policies,* edited by Arnold R. Weber et al. Madison, Wis.: Industrial Relations Research Association.

Capelli, Peter, and Peter Sherer. 1990. "Assessing Worker Attitudes Under a Two-Tier Wage Plan." *Industrial and Labor Relations Review* 43 (January): 225–44.

Carnoy, Martin, and Derek Shearer. 1980. *Economic Democracy: The Challenge of the 1980s.* Armonk, N.Y.: M. E. Sharpe.

Chamberlain, Neil. 1951. *Collective Bargaining.* New York: McGraw-Hill.

Chenery, Hollis, and T. N. Srinivasan. 1988. *Handbook of Development Economics.* Amsterdam: North Holland.

Clague, Ewan, and Leo Kramer. 1976. *Manpower Policies and Programs: A Review.* Kalamazoo, Mich.: Upjohn Institute.

Collier, R. B., and D. Collier. 1979. "Inducements versus Constraints: Disaggregating 'Corporatism'." *American Political Science Review* 73 (December): 967–86.

Commons, John R. 1913. "American Shoemakers, 1648–1895." In *Labor and Administration.* New York: Macmillan Co.

Commons, John R. 1961. Reprint. *Institutional Economics.* Madison: University of Wisconsin Press. Original edition, New York: Macmillan, 1934.

Cooke, William, and David Meyer. 1990. "Structural and Market Predictors of Corporate Labor Relations Strategies." *Industrial and Labor Relations Review* 43 (January): 280–93.

Cornfield, Daniel. 1991. "The Attitude of Employee Association Members Toward Union Mergers: The Effect of Socioeconomic Status." *Industrial and Labor Relations Review* 44 (January): 334–48.

Coser, Lewis A. 1956. *The Functions of Social Conflict.* Glencoe, Ill.: Free Press.

Csikszentmihalyi, Mihaly. 1993. *The Evolving Self: A Psychology for the Third Millenium.* New York: HarperCollins.

Dahl, Robert A. 1970. *After the Revolution.* New Haven: Yale University Press.

Dahrendorf, Ralf. 1959. *Class and Class Conflict in Industrial Society.* Stanford: Stanford University Press.

Deming, W. Edwards. 1951. *Elementary Principles of the Statistical Control of Quality.* Nippon: Kagaku Gijutsu Renmei JUSE.

Derber, Milton. 1988. "Management Organization for Collective Bargaining in the Public Sector." In *Public Sector Bargaining,* edited by B. Aaron, J. M. Najita, and J. L. Stern. Washington, D.C.: Bureau of National Affairs, Inc.

Doeringer, P., and M. Piore. 1971. *Internal Labor Markets and Manpower Analysis.* Lexington, Mass.: Heath.

Dunlop, John. T. 1944. *Wage Determination under Trade Unions.* New York: Macmillan.

Dunlop, John T. 1958. *Industrial Relations Systems.* New York: Holt, Rinehart, and Winston.

Dunlop, John T., et al. 1975. *Industrialism and Industrial Man Reconsidered.* Princeton: Interuniversity Study of Human Resources in National Development.

Dunnett, M. D., ed. 1976. *Handbook of Industrial and Organizational Psychology.* Chicago: Rand McNally.

Durkheim, Emile. 1933. *The Division of Labor in Society.* New York: Macmillan.

Durkheim, Emile. 1958. *The Rule of Sociological Method.* Edited by George E. G. Catlin. Translated by Sarah A Solovay and John H. Mueller. Glencoe, Ill.: Free Press.

Easton, David. 1965. *A Systems Analysis of Political Life.* New York: Wiley.

Edwards, Richard C., Michael Reich, and David M. Gordon. 1975. *Labor Market Segmentation.* Lexington: Heath.

Eilbert, H. 1959. "The Development of Personnel Management in the United States." *Business History Review* 33:345–64.

Farber, Henry S., and Alan B. Krueger. 1993. "Union Membership in the United States: The Decline Continues." In *Employee Representation: Alternatives and Futures,* edited by Bruce E. Kaufman and Morris M. Kleiner. Madison, Wis.: Industrial Relations Research Association.

Flanders, Allen. 1965. *Industrial Relations.* London: Faber.

Fox, Alan. 1973. "Industrial Relations: A Social Critique of Pluralism." In *Man and Organization,* edited by J. Child. London: Allen and Unwin.

Freeman, Richard, and James Medoff. 1984. *What Do Unions Do?* New York: Basic Books.

Galbraith, J. K. 1967. *The New Industrial State.* Boston: Houghton Mifflin.

Gallagher, Daniel E., and George Srauss. 1991. "Union Membership Attitudes and Participation." In *The State of the Union,* edited by G. Strauss et al. Madison, Wis.: Industrial Relations Research Association.

Garfinkel, Harold. 1967. *Studies in Ethnomethodology.* Englewood Cliffs, N.J.: Prentice-Hall.

Gilbertson, H. S. 1950. *Personnel Policies and Unionism.* Boston: Ginn.

Goldfield, Michael. 1989. "Worker Insurgency, Radical Organization, and New Deal Labor Legislation." *American Political Science Review* 83 (December): 1257–1282.

Goldman, R. B. 1976. *A Work Experiment: Six Americans in a Swedish Plant.* New York: Ford Foundation.

Gordon, M. E., and A. J. Nurick. 1981. "Psychological Approaches to the Study of Unions and Union-Management Relations." *Psychological Bulletin* 90, no. 2:293–306.

Gorz, Andre. 1967. *A Strategy for Labor.* Boston: Beacon Press.

Granovetter, Mark. 1974. *Getting a Job.* Cambridge, Mass.: Harvard University Press.

Granovetter, Mark, and Charles Tilly. 1988. "Inequality and Labor Processes." In *Handbook of Sociology,* edited by N. J. Smelser. Newbury Park, Calif.: Sage.

Greenberg, J. 1992. "The Social Side of Fairness: Interpersonal and Informational Classes of Organizational Justice." In *Justice in the Workplace: Approaching Fairness in Human Resource Management,* edited by R. Cropanzano. Hillsdale, N.J.: Erlbaum.

Greenfield, Patricia A., and Robert J. Pleasure. 1993. "Representatives of their Own Choosing: Finding Workers' Voice in the Legitimacy and Power of their Unions." In *Employee Representation: Alternatives and Futures,* edited by Bruce E. Kaufman and Morris M. Kleiner. Madison, Wis.: Industrial Relations Research Association.

Hackman, J. Richard, and Mary D. Lee. 1979. *Redesigning Work: A Strategy for Change.* Scarsdale N.Y.: Work in America Institute.

Hackman, J. Richard, and Greg R. Oldham. 1975. "Development of the Job Diagnostic Survey." *Journal of Applied Psychology* 60, no. 2:159–70.

Hamer, Tove, and David L. Wazeter. 1993. "Dimensions of Local Union Effectiveness." *Industrial and Labor Relations Review* 46 (January): 302–19

Healy, James J. 1965. *Creative Collective Bargaining.* Englewood Cliffs, N.J.: Prentice Hall.

Heilbroner, Robert. 1974. *An Inquiry into the Human Prospect.* New York: Norton.

Heilbroner, Robert. 1980. *An Inquiry into the Human Prospect Updated for the 1980s.* New York: Norton.

Hirschhorn, L. 1984. *Beyond Mechanization.* Cambridge, Mass.: MIT Press.

Hirschman, A. 1970. *Exit, Voice and Loyalty.* Cambridge, Mass.: Harvard University Press.

Homans, George. 1964. "Bringing Men Back In." *American Sociological Review* 29:809–18.

Hsieh, Ching-Yao, and Stephen L. Mangum. 1986. *A Search for Synthesis in Economic Theory.* Armonk, N.Y.: M. E. Sharpe.

Hyman, Richard. 1975. *Industrial Relations: A Marxist Introduction.* London: Macmillan.

Ichniowski, B. C. 1986. "The Effects of Grievance Activity on Productivity." *Industrial and Labor Relations Review* 40:75–89.

Jacoby, Sanford. 1985. *Employing Bureaucracy: Managers, Unions, and the Transformation of Work in American Industry, 1900–1945.* New York: Columbia University Press.

Jacoby, Sanford. 1988a. "Employee Attitude Surveys in Historical Perspective." *Industrial Relations* 27:74–93.

Jacoby, Sanford. 1988b. "The Intellectual Foundations of Industrial Relations." Working Paper, November. Los Angeles, Calif.: University of California.

Jacoby, Sanford. 1993. "Review Symposium: The Origins and Evolution of the Field of Industrial Relations in the United States." *Industrial and Labor Relations Review* 46 (January): 399–403.

Jensen, Michael. 1983. "Organization Theory and Methodology." *Accounting Review* 50 (April): 319–39.

Jensen, Michael, and William Meckling. 1976. "Theory of the Firm: Managerial Behavior, Agency Costs, and Capital Structure." *Journal of Financial Economics* 3 (October): 305–60.

Jurgens, Ulrich, et al. 1993. "The Transformation of Industrial Relations in Eastern Germany." *Industrial and Labor Relations Review* 46 (January): 229–44.

Kaestle, P. 1990. "A New Rationale for Organizational Structure. *Planning Review* 16:20–27.

Kaufman, Bruce. 1989. "Models of Man in Industrial Relations Research." *Industrial and Labor Relations Review* 43 (October): 72–88.

Kaufman, Bruce. 1993. *The Origin and Evolution of the Field of Industrial Relations in the United States.* Ithaca, N.Y.: ILR Press.

Kaufman, R. T. 1992. "The Effects of Improshare on Productivity." *Industrial and Labor Relations Review* 45:311–22.

Kerr, Clark. 1954. "The Balkanization of Labor Markets." In *Labor Mobility and Economic Opportunity,* edited by E. Wight Bakke et al. Cambridge and New York: Technology Press of the Massachusetts Institute of Technology and John Wiley & Sons.

Kerr, Clark, John Dunlop, Frederick Harbison, and Charles Myers. 1960. *Industrialism and Industrial Man.* Cambridge, Mass.: Harvard University Press.

Kochan, Tom. 1974. "A Theory of Multilateral Bargaining in City Governments." *Industrial and Labor Relations Review* 27:525–42.

Kochan, Tom. 1980. *Collective Bargaining and Industrial Relations.* Homewood, Ill.: Irwin.

Kochan, Tom, Harry Katz, and Robert McKersie. 1986. *The Transformation of American Industrial Relations.* New York: Basic Books.

Kuruvilla, Sarosh, Daniel Gallagher, and Kurt Wetzel. 1993. "The Development of Members' Attitudes toward their Unions: Sweden and Canada." *Industrial and Labor Relations Review* 46 (April): 499–514.

Kuznets, Simon. 1955. "Economic Growth and Income Inequality." *American Economic Review* 45 (March): 1–28.

Lane, Christel. 1989. *Management and Labour in Europe: The Industrial Enterprise in Germany, Britain and France.* Brookfield, Vt.: Gower Publishing.

Lewicki, R. B. Sheppard, and M. Bazerman, eds. 1986. *Research on Negotiation in Organizations.* Greenwich, Conn.: JAI Press.

Lewicki, R. J., and J. A. Litterer. 1985. *Negotiation.* Homewood, Ill.: Irwin.

Lindblom, Charles. 1977. *Politics and Markets: The World's Political-Economic Systems.* New York: Basic Books.

Lippman, Steven A., and John J. McCall. 1976. "The Economics of Job Search: A Survey." *Economic Inquiry* 14 (June): 155–89.

Locke, E. A. 1976. "The Nature and Causes of Job Satisfaction." In *Handbook of Industrial and Organizational Psychology,* edited by M. D. Dunnette. Chicago: Rand McNally.

Mangum, Stephen L. 1989. "Evidence on Private Sector Training." In *Investing in People: A Strategy to Address America's Work Force Crisis.* Washington, D.C.: U.S. Department of Labor, Commission on Workforce Quality and Labor Market Efficiency.

Margerison, C. J. 1969, "What Do We Mean by Industrial Relations: A Behavioral Science Approach." *British Journal of Industrial Relations* 7 (July): 273–86.

Maslow, A. H. 1970. *Motivation and Personality.* 2d ed. New York: Harper and Row.

Mayo, Elton. 1945. *The Social Problem of an Industrial Civilization.* Boston: Harvard University Press.

McNulty, Paul J. 1980. *The Origins and Development of Labor Economics.* Cambridge, Mass.: MIT Press.

Meier, Gerald. 1984. *Leading Issues in Economic Development.* 4th ed. New York: Oxford University Press

Miceli, Marcia, Janet Near, and Charles Schwenk. 1991. "Who Blows the Whistle and Why?" *Industrial and Labor Relations Review* 45 (October): 113–30.

Miller, Delbert C., and William H. Form. 1980. *Industrial Sociology: Work in Organizational Life.* 3rd ed. New York: Harper and Row.

Mincer, Jacob. 1958. "Investment in Human Capital and Personal Income Distribution." *Journal of Political Economy* 56 (August): 281–302.

Mincer, Jacob. 1962. "On-the-Job-Training: Costs, Returns, and Some Implications." *Journal of Political Economy* 70 (October): pt. 2.

Mintzberg, Henry. 1983. *Structure in Fives: Designing Effective Organizations.* Englewood Cliffs, N.J.: Prentice Hall.

Mirrlees, J. A. 1976. "The Optimal Structure of Incentives and Authority within an Organization." *Bell Journal of Economics* 7 (Spring): 105–31.

Montgomery, Ruth. 1989. "The Influence of Attitudes and Normative Pressures on Voting Decisions in a Union Certification Election." *Industrial and Labor Relations Review* 42 (January): 262–79.

Munsterberg, H. 1913. *Psychology and Industrial Efficiency.* Boston: Houghton-Mifflin.

Nelson, Daniel. 1975. *Managers and Workers: Origins of the New Factory System in the United States, 1880–1920.* Madison: University of Wisconsin Press.

Osterman, Paul. 1988. *Employment Futures: Reorganization, Dislocation, and Public Policy.* New York: Oxford University Press.

Osterman, Paul. 1994. "How Common Is Workplace Transformation and Who Adopts It?" *Industrial and Labor Relations Review* 47 (January): 173–88.

Parkin, Frank. 1979. *Marxism and Class Theory: A Bourgeois Critique.* London: Tavistock Publications.

Parsons, Talcott. 1951. *The Social System.* Glencoe, Ill.: Free Press.

Parsons, Talcott. 1959. "Some Problems Confronting Sociology as a Profession." *American Sociological Review* 29:547–59.

Perlman, Selig. 1949. *A Theory of the Labor Movement.* New York: Kelley.

Petersen, P. B. 1990. "Fighting for a Better Navy: An Attempt at Scientific Management (1905–1912)." *Journal of Management* 16:151–66.

Piore, Michael. 1977. "The Dual Labor Market: Theory and Implications." In *Problems in Political Economy: An Urban Perspective,* edited by D. M. Gordon. Lexington: Heath.

Polanyi, Karl. 1957. Reprint. *The Great Transformation: The Political and Economic Origins of Our Time.* Boston: Beacon Press. Original edition, New York: Farrar and Rinehart, 1944.

Porter, Lyman, and Edward Lawler. 1968. Managerial Attitudes and Performance. Homewood, Ill.: R. D. Irwin.

Prebisch, Raul. 1959. "Commercial Policy in the Underdeveloped Countries." *American Economic Review, Papers and Proceedings* 49 (May): 251–73.

Ready, Kathryn. 1990. "Is Pattern Bargaining Dead?" *Industrial and Labor Relations Review* 43 (January): 272–79.

Resnick, Stephen A., and Richard D. Wolff. 1987. *Knowledge and Class: A Marxian Critique of Political Economy.* Chicago: University of Chicago Press.

Roethlisberger, F. J., and William J. Dickson. 1939. *Management and the Worker.* Cambridge, Mass.: Harvard University Press.

Ross, A. M. 1966. *Industrial Relations and Economic Development.* New York: Macmillan for the International Institute for Labour Studies, Geneva, Switzerland.

Ross, A. M., and P. T. Hartman. 1960. *Changing Patterns of Industrial Conflict.* New York: Wiley.

Rostow, Walter. 1960. *The Stages of Economic Growth.* Cambridge, Cambridge University Press.

Roy, Donald. 1952. "Restriction of Output in a Piecework Machine Shop." Ph.D. dissertation, University of Chicago.

Samuels, Warren J. 1966. *The Classical Theory of Economic Policy.* Cleveland: World Publishing Co.

Sayles, L. R., and G. Strauss. 1967. *The Local Union.* New York: Harcourt, Brace, and World.

Schmitter, P. C., and G. Lehmbruch. 1979. *Trends Toward Corporatist Intermediation.* Beverly Hills, Calif.: Sage Publications.

Schmitter, Philippe. 1979. "Still the Century of Corporatism." In *Trends Toward Corporatist Intermediation,* edited by P. C. Schmitter and G. Lehmbruch. Beverly Hills, Calif.: Sage Publications.

Schumpeter, Joseph. 1950. *Capitalism, Socialism, and Democracy.* New York: Harper.

Schur, Lisa, and Douglas Kruse. 1992. "Gender Differences in Attitudes Toward Unions." *Industrial and Labor Relations Review* 46 (October): 89–102.

Schwab, D. P., S. L. Rynes, and R. J. Aldag. 1987. "Theories and Research on Job Search and Choice." *Research in Personnel and Human Resource Management* 5:129–66.

Seeman, M. 1975. "Alienation Studies." *Annual Review of Sociology* 1:91–124.

Shaw, Bernard. 1889. *Fabian Essays in Socialism.* London: W. Scott.

Skinner, B. F. 1971. *Beyond Freedom and Dignity.* New York: Bantam Books.

Smelser, Neil J. 1988. Introduction to *Handbook of Sociology,* edited by N. J. Smelser. Newbury Park, Calif.: Sage.

Smith, Adam. 1776. *Wealth of Nations.* Reprinted 1922, London: J. M. Dent & Sons.

Somers, Gerald. 1968. *Essays in Industrial Relations Theory.* Ames, Iowa: Iowa State University Press.

Stein, Bruno. 1980. "Public Income Maintenance Systems in America." In *Social Security and Pensions in Transition.* New York: Free Press, 1980.

Stevens, Carl. 1963. *Strategy and Collective Bargaining Negotiations.* New York: McGraw-Hill.

Storey, John. 1983. *Managerial Prerogative and the Question of Control.* London: Routledge and Kegan Paul.

Straka, John. 1993. "Is Poor Worker Morale Costly to Firms?" *Industrial and Labor Relations Review* 46 (January): 381–94.

Strauss, George. 1977. "Union Government in the U.S.: Research Past and Future." *Industrial Relations* 16, no. 2:215–42.

Sturmthal, Adolph. 1972. *Comparative Labor Movements.* Belmont, Calif.: Wadsworth.

Tannenbaum, Frank. 1952. *A Philosophy of Labor.* New York: Knopf.

Taylor, W. Frederick. 1911. *Principles of Scientific Management.* New York: Harper.

Thompson, Kenneth. 1980. "The Organizational Society." In *Control and Ideology in Organizations,* edited by G. Salaman and K. Thompson. Cambridge, Mass.: MIT Press.

Thompson, Paul. 1989. *The Nature of Work: An Introduction to Debates on the Labour Process.* 2d ed. London: Macmillan.

Thurow, Lester. 1972. "A Job Competition Model." In *The American Distribution of Income; A Structural Problem,* edited by L. Thurow and R. E. B. Lucas. Study for Joint Economic Committee of the Congress. Washington, D.C.: Government Printing Office.

Tucker, Robert C. 1978. *The Marx-Engels Reader.* New York: W. W. Norton.

Turner, J. H. 1982. *The Structure of Sociological Theory.* Homewood, Ill.: Dorsey Press.

Verma, A., and R. B. McKersie. 1987. "Employee Involvement: The Implications of Noninvolvement by Unions." *Industrial and Labor Relations Review* 40:556–68.

Vroom, V. H. 1964. *Work and Motivation.* New York: Wiley.

Waldo, Dwight. 1975. "Political Science: Tradition, Discipline, Profession, Science, Enterprise." In *Handbook of Political Science,* edited by F. Greenstein and N. Polsby. Vol. 1. New York: Addison-Wesley.

Wallerstein, Michael. 1989. "Union Organization in Advanced Industrial Democracies." *American Political Science Review* 83 (February): 481–501.

Wallerstein, Michael. 1990. "Centralized Bargaining and Wage Restraint." *American Journal of Political Science* 34, no. 4:982–1004.

Walton, Richard, and Robert McKersie. 1965. *A Behavioral Theory of Labor Negotiations.* New York: McGraw-Hill.

Webb, Sidney, and Beatrice Webb. 1897. *Industrial Democracy.* London: Longman Green.

Weber, Arnold, et al. 1969. *Public-Private Manpower Policies.* Madison, Wis.: Industrial Relations Research Association.

Weintraub, Sidney. 1978. *Capitalism's Inflation and Unemployment Crisis.* Reading, Mass.: Addison-Wesley.

Wever, Kirsten. 1989. "Toward a Structural Account of Union Participation in Management: the Case of Western Airlines." *Industrial and Labor Relations Review* 42 (July): 600–609.

Wheeler, Hoyt. 1985. *Industrial Conflict: An Integrative Theory.* Columbia: University of South Carolina Press.

Wheeler, Hoyt N., and John A. McClendon. 1991. "The Individual Decision to Unionize." In *The State of the Unions,* edited by G. Strauss et al. Madison, Wis.: Industrial Relations Research Association.

Whyte, William Foote. 1987. "From Human Relations to Organizational Behavior." *Industrial and Labor Relations Review* 40 (July): 487–500.

Williamson, Oliver E. 1985. *The Economic Institutions of Capitalism.* New York: Free Press.

Wilson, Edmund O. 1975. *Sociology: The New Synthesis.* Cambridge, Mass: Harvard University Press.

Wrong, Dennis. 1961. "The Oversocialized Conception of Man in Modern Sociology." *American Sociological Review* 26:183–93.

Yankelovich, Daniel. 1981. *New Rules.* New York: Random House.

Zeuthen, Frederick. 1930. *Problems of Monopoly and Economic Welfare.* London: G. Routledge and Sons.

INDEX

AARP (American Association for Retired Person), 34
Actors, in social system, 62–63, 73–75, 80–82, 99–100
Adams, Roy, 2, 87–88
Affirmative action policies, 25
Agency shops, 27
Agent(s), 14–16, 32, 82, 88–89, 114, 139; agency problem, 92, 102–3, 107; institutions as, 34–35, 55, 62, 90; labor unions as, 14, 88–89, 104, 107, 109; need for, 22–23, 133, 140, 146; satisfaction with, 129–30. *See also individual institutions and organizations*
Aggression, inherent tendency toward, 70, 128
Agriculture, 8, 37, 140–41, 143, 144–45
Alienation, 9, 42, 54–55, 114–15, 124–26, 128
Allocation of human resources/labor, 12, 24–28, 31, 48, 53, 56–57; classical economics emphasis on, 37, 39, 56–57, 58; institutionalist emphasis on, 37, 44–45, 94; Marxism's de-emphasis, 40, 56; negotiation issues in, 134–35, 142; in third-world economics, 144–45
Amalgamated Clothing and Textile Workers (ACTWU), 102
American Association for Retired Person (AARP), 34
American institutional economics. *See* Institutional labor economics;

Wisconsin School institutionalism
Antidiscrimination legislation, 94
Apprenticeships, 12, 22, 24, 133
Argentina, corporatism, 17, 81
Assembly-line technology, 126–27, 128
Attitudes, individual, 118–21, 123, 130. *See also* Alienation
Authoritarianism, 16–17, 35
Authority, 35, 59, 71–73, 77, 80–88, 106–7, 111
Autonomy, 117, 119–20, 122, 125–30, 135–36

Bakke, E. Wight, 97–98
Barbash, Jack, 43, 91, 111, 148n.2
Bargaining, 2, 25, 65, 74–77, 135, 148n.2; pluralist focus on, 67, 70–71; systems in Asia and Europe, 141–42; transactions, 43, 94. *See also* Collective bargaining
Becker, Gary, 97
Behavior, group, 10, 129–30; organizational, 5, 65–66, 115
Behavior, individual, 10, 69–70, 78, 89, 101, 115; control in scientific management, 121–22; institutionalist interpretation, 92, 104, 107; political science defined in terms of, 82–83; systems theory approach, 62, 66–67, 69; technological change effects, 126–28. *See also* Conflict
Behaviorism, 61, 69, 120, 122
Biology, behavior seen as determined by, 69–70, 89

Bottom-up methodology, 11–12
Bourgeoisie. *See* Capitalism and capitalists; Class(es)
Burawoy, Michael, 66–67, 75–76
Business firm(s), 1, 12, 17, 34–35, 73–75, 92, 146; control, 21, 23–24, 42, 133–34, 139, 141; human resource activities, 12, 25–28, 77, 135–39; institution as synonymous term, 104; personnel department, 47, 123–24; scientific management application, 121–22; training programs sponsored by, 21–22, 133–34; viewed as governments, 82–83. *See also* Capitalism; Management

Capital, 30, 63, 102, 108, 135–36; as social relation of production, 51–52; in third-world economies, 145–46
Capitalism and capitalists, 13–14, 19, 27–28, 35, 38, 99; for Granovetter and Tilly, 73–75; Marxism on, 9, 37, 39–41, 50–58, 62–63, 136; New Deal legislation effects on, 79–80
Central planning, 9–10, 16–17, 19–20, 30, 35, 72; in Marxist socialism, 55–56
Clague, Ewan, 97
Class(es), 63–64, 67–68, 110, 117, 132–34, 136; classical economics view, 56, 58; conflict, 9, 18, 20, 64; institutionalist de-emphasis, 1, 109–10; Marxist theory, 9, 18, 20, 37, 52–55, 58, 78
Classical economics, 37–39, 53, 90–92, 132; of Adam Smith, 7, 13, 16, 57, 58, 90–91; compared with Marxism, 39–41, 56–59; on market system, 7, 13, 17–18; reactions to, 41–42, 45–46, 91–92, 93–94, 112. *See also* Neoclassical economics
Closed shops, 27, 28
Collective action, 4–5, 32, 93, 94, 129. *See also* Collective bargaining
Collective bargaining, 4, 51, 96, 118, 141–42; institutionalist emphasis on, 44–45, 46, 91, 101; management's

rights and power in, 25, 46, 135; right to, 84, 87–88, 147n.1. *See also* Bargaining
Commons, John R., 1–2, 4, 32, 99, 109–11, 119; contribution to institutionalism, 41–43, 91–92, 93–95; influence, 96–97, 112; on market controls, 117
Communism, 10, 72. *See also* Central planning; Marx and Marxism
Communist countries, former, 8, 9–10, 11, 16–17, 79
Company towns, 33
Comparable worth policies, 25–26, 135
Compensation, 25–27, 29, 93–94. *See also* Wage rates/wages
Competitive market. *See* Free market
Comprehensive Employment and Training Act (U.S., 1973), 96
Computerization, 127, 148n.47
Conflict, 2, 5–6, 23–25, 32, 42, 132–33; biological explanation, 69–70; classical economics approach, 8–10; as industrial life characteristic, 116, 128; Marxist approach to, 9–10; political science theory focusing on, 79, 88; resolution, 5–6, 28, 65, 77, 99, 102–3, 121; sociological approaches to, 70–76, 89
Contract(s), 3–4, 14, 18, 26, 30, 83–84; effects on job choice, 116–17; implicit, 44–45, 103; for institutionalists, 42, 91, 93; Marx on, 51; for neo-institutionalists, 104–6, 108–9
Control, 3–5, 66, 118–22, 125, 128, 130; autocratic, 8; centers of, 15–16, 20, 131–32, 139, 140–42, 146. *See also* Business firm(s); Government; Management; Market, the; classical economics on, 91; in employment relations, 10–19, 34–36; governance structure as form of, 107; in human resource management, 25–28, 27, 31–34, 121–24, 133, 135–38; issues of in psychological perspective, 114, 116–18, 121, 128, 248nn.2, 3; Marxism on, 18, 42, 55; negotiation over, 43,

59; over production, 45, 75, 84–85; pluralist focus on, 38, 46; political science theory on, 77, 79; resistance to, 126, 128; role in workers' need for agents, 88–89; shared, 18, 19, 21 *table,* 23–24; in voucher-based education system, 22
Convergence hypothesis, 98, 101, 141–42, 144
Cooke, William, 65
Cooperation in labor-management relations, 101–3
Corporatist state, 17, 80–82
Coser, Lewis, 71, 72–73
Courts: insurance litigation, 138–39; reasonable value establishment, 93, 95
Craft unions, apprenticeships, 133
Csikszentmihalyi, Mihaly, 127–28, 131–32
Culture, 7; estrangement from, 125; relationship to employment relations, hypotheses on, 98, 101, 141–42
Customary procedure, 85, 95

Dahl, Robert A., 85, 87, 108, 109
Dahrendorf, Ralf, 71–73
Decentralization, 35, 45, 127, 131, 135
Decision making: decentralization, 45; participation in, 12, 65, 86–88, 91, 101–2
Deductive methodology, 40
Demand side of the market. *See* Supply and demand
Democratic institutions, 17, 20, 35, 110–11
Dependency theory, on third-world economic development, 143
Depression, Great, 79, 137–38
Developing countries. *See* Third world
Development of human resources/labor, 12, 20–24, 31, 53–54, 56; negotiation issues in, 133–34, 142. *See also* Training
Dialectical theories on conflict, 70
Dickens, Charles, 7

Differentiation, 131–32, 134
Disability insurance, 137–38
Discrimination, 74–75, 93–94, 116, 133; attempts to remedy, 24–25
Divine right, authority based on, 85–86
Dualism, in third-world economic development, 142–43, 145
Dunlop, John T., 3–4, 10, 41, 50, 92, 98–101
Durkheim, Emile, 63, 64–66, 73, 89

Economic development, 57–58, 98–99, 100, 112–13; in third world, 142–46
Economic growth, 95–96, 98, 102–3, 139, 142; classical economics focus on, 39, 90–91; third-world, 142–46
Economic Institutions of Capitalism, The (Williamson), 104
Economics, 1–2, 4, 10–11, 32, 61, 69; as element in industrial relations field, 48–49; functionalism in, 63. *See also individual schools*
Education, 12, 21–22, 61, 133–34. *See also* Training
Efficiency, 47, 104, 118, 121–23; sought by classical economists, 37, 39, 90
Electric power, effects of shift to from steam power, 126–28
Employee-assistance programs, 12, 32–33, 124, 138
Employment, 17–18, 25–27, 33, 44, 73–74, 123; full, 30–31; hiring practices, 25–28, 93–94, 123, 135; state services, 12; in third world, 142–43. *See also* Jobs; Unemployment
Equilibrium (Stability), 62, 70–71, 100–101, 132
European Economic Community (EEC), 95–96, 98
European institutionalism. *See* Pluralism
Evolutionary change, 9, 38, 68
Expectancy theory, on job dissatisfaction, 125–26
Exploitation, 55, 127–29, 132, 134–35; Marxist focus on, 9, 37, 40, 43, 114, 136

Fabianism, 45–46, 92, 110–11
Farmers unions, in third world, 143
Featherbedding, 30
Feelings, 32, 114–16, 128, 129
Firms. *See* Business firm(s)
Flanders, Allen, 3, 4, 92
Fox, Alan, 46
Free (Competitive) market, 7–10, 13–14, 27, 56, 126, 129; classical economic theory focus on, 7, 37, 39, 58–59, 90; as source of labor-management conflict, 42. *See also* Classical economics; Market, the
Friedman, Milton, 13
Functionalism, 62–63, 62–68, 70–71

Garment industry, union role in strategic decisions, 102
Germany, 69, 88, 109, 141–42
Gilbertson, H. S., 123
Global economy. *See* International economy
Gordon, M. E., 119
Governance structures, 92, 105–9, 111, 112. *See also* Grievance procedures; Wage rates
Government, 58, 85–86, 89, 129, 140
    as actor in social system, 62, 73, 99–100
    control centered in, 13, 20–22, 35, 45, 55, 139, 142
    employment relations role, 10–12, 14–17, 19, 34–35, 96, 111; in corporatist state, 81–82; regulations on personnel policies, 124; for Wisconsin School, 42–43
    human resource activities, 12, 21–22, 25–34, 96–98, 133–34, 136–38
    Marxism on, 51, 54
    role in third-world economic development, 145–46
Granovetter, Mark, 73–75, 76, 136–37
Grievance procedures, 29, 105–7, 118, 137; union role, 25, 91, 135
Growth, economic. *See* Economic growth

Hamer, Tove, 65–66
Harbison, Frederick, 4, 92, 98, 101
Harmony, 64, 66, 118–23, 127–28, 132, 134; as condition for economic growth, 91, 93, 94, 114
Hartman, P. T., 98
Hawthorne Studies, 119–21, 123
Health insurance, 8, 32–34, 138
Healy, James J., 101
Hearing process, in worker's compensation, 138–39
Hierarchy, as nature of corporatism, 81
Hiring. *See* Employment
Hiring halls, 27, 28, 135
Hirschhorn, L., 126, 127
Hobbes, Thomas, 78
Homans, George, 69, 89
HRM. *See* Human resource management
Hsieh, Ching-Yao, 90–91, 147n.1
Human capital theory, 22–24, 57, 97
Human relations school, 38, 47, 48, 119–21, 137. *See also* Human resource management
Human resource activities, 5, 12–20. *See also* Allocation; Development; Maintenance; Utilization
Human resource management (HRM), 31, 38, 46–48, 81–82, 115, 137; distrust of, 119, 136; professional managers trained in, 123–24; systems theory use, 64
Human resource management department, 124. *See also* Personnel administration
Hyman, Richard, 4–5, 66

Implicit contracts, 44–45, 103
Import substitution, 143
Incentive pay plans, proposal for, 47
Income distribution: and third-world economic development, 142–46, 148n.3. *See also* Wage rates/wages
Indentured servants, 22
Industrial age, 5, 7, 41, 139, 141–42. *See also* Technology

Industrial and Labor Relations Review
(period.), 129
Industrial Commission, Wisconsin, 95
Industrial democracy, 20, 91–92
Industrial Democracy (Webb and Webb),
110–11
Industrialization, 68, 99–100, 141–46,
148n.3; and logic of industrialism, 68;
relationship to culture, hypotheses on,
98, 101, 141–42. *See also* Industrial
revolution; Technology
Industrial relations (field and theory), 1,
3–5, 10–19, 59–60, 70; and economic
development theory, 98–99, 144–46;
on human resource activities, 22–34,
136; Marxist and non-Marxist
compared, 50, 53–55; systems theory
use, 62, 64, 65–67, 69–73. *See also*
Social science; *individual schools of
thought*
Industrial Relations Research Association (IRRA), 97, 129
Industrial Relations Systems (Dunlop), 99
Industrial revolution, 7–8, 37–38, 41, 126,
139–41. *See also* Industrialization
Industrial society. *See* Industrialization;
Society
Information, 21 *table,* 22, 27; decentralization of, 127; sophisticated systems,
131
Insecurity, 8, 114, 126, 127, 134–35,
142. *See also* Security
Institutional economics, 1–5, 10, 37–38,
41, 47–49, 101–9, 147n.1; dissent
from traditional economic theory, 61,
91–92; European and American
compared, 109–13; on harmony, 119,
132; on human resource activities,
134, 137–39; psychological issues'
role in, 114, 130. *See also* Institutional labor economics; Pluralism;
Wisconsin School institutionalism
Institutional Economics (Commons), 93–
95
Institutional labor economics, 37–38, 41–
45, 49, 92, 94–103, 112. *See also*

Institutional economics
Institutions, 3–4, 12, 34–36, 59, 69, 115;
as actors in social system, 62, 99–
100; change in, fundamental
determination of, 100–101. *See also*
Institutional economics; Protective
institutions; *individual institutions*
Insurance, 8, 32–34, 43, 137–38. *See
also* Social insurance; Unemploy-
ment
Integration, 64, 131–32, 134
Interest, community of, 93, 119
Internal labor markets, 2, 26–28
International (Global; World) economy,
71–73, 80–82, 95–98, 139, 142–46;
trade, 39, 81–82, 95–96, 143–44,
148n.4
International Ladies Garment Workers
Union (ILGWU), 102
Investment, 10, 136
"Invisible hand" concept, 91

Jacoby, Sanford, 1
Japan, 141
Job market. *See* Labor market
Jobs, 3–4, 12, 54, 73–74, 148n.1;
dissatisfaction, 125, 126; information,
control over, 21–22, 27; ladders, 106;
mobility, 9, 25, 96, 97–98; queue, 44,
94, 133; satisfaction, 2, 25, 87; skills,
8, 17–18, 24, 57, 104–6, 133. *See also*
Employment; Security; Training
Job search theory, 27
Job Training Partnership Act (U.S.,
1982), 96
Johnson, Lyndon B., 23, 97
Justice, 37, 125–26
Just-in-time inventory systems, 131

Katz, Harry, 102–3
Kaufman, Bruce, 61, 114–15, 130
Kaufman, R. T., 38
Kerr, Clark, 41, 92, 97, 98, 101, 141
Kochan, Tom, 102–3
Kramer, Leo, 97
Kuznets, Simon, 143, 148n.3

Labor, 5, 7, 10–20, 40, 96; as actor in social system, 62, 99–100; and the corporatist state, 80–82; New Deal legislation effects, 79–80; oversupply of, 8–9; relations with management, 38, 93, 101–3; supplies in third world, 144–45; value, 39–40. *See also* Allocation; Development; Labor movement; Labor problem(s); Maintenance; Utilization; Workers

Labor, division of, 99; Marx on, 53, 54–55, 57–58, 125

Labor, U.S. Dept. of, 16

Labor economics, 1, 73

Labor federation, under corporatism, 81

Labor-management committees, 12, 14, 30–31, 101–3, 112, 138–39. *See also* Works councils

Labor (Job) market, 12, 41–44, 94, 97–99, 116; internal, 2, 27–28

Labor Market Board, 23, 96, 97

Labor movement(s), 34–35, 79–80, 98, 110–11, 119–20, 141–42. *See also* Labor unions; Unions

Labor problem(s), 37, 38, 119–21, 126–29; Hawthorne effect applied to, 98; from individual perspective, 115–17; in third world, 142–46

Labor unions, 1–3, 25, 35, 65–66, 105–6, 118; as agents, 14, 88–89, 104, 107, 109; apprenticeship programs, 22, 24, 130; control centered in, 13, 17, 19, 128; control of, 14–15, 148n.2; development of, 5, 68, 140–41; disillusionment regarding, 129; human resource activities, 23–28, 30, 33, 133, 135–36, 138; importance for Fabianism, 45–46; institutionalist thought on, 43, 91, 99, 112–13; as possible governance structures, 87; as protective institutions, 8, 43, 99; psychological studies of, 129; relationships with political movements, 79; in third world, 146. *See also* Labor-management committees; Labor movement

Labour Party, British, 110

Laissez faire economics, 91

Land reform, in third world, 143

Latin America, 17, 81

Less-developed countries. *See* Third world

Leviathan (Hobbes), 78

Lewis, W. Arthur, 144–45

Lobbying, 77, 80

London School of Economics, 110

Loyalty, employee, 137

McDonald, James Ramsey, 45

Machiavelli, 77–78

McKersie, Robert, 102–3

McNulty, Paul J., 97

Macro-economics, 10, 30–31

Maintenance of human resources/labor, 12, 31–34, 53, 55–56, 112, 141; negotiational issues, 137–39, 142; in third-world economies, 145

Majority rule, 85–86

Malthus, Thomas, 90

Management, 10–11, 25, 46–48, 69, 117, 131; as actor in social system, 62, 99–100; authority, 80–88; control centered in, 14, 20, 83, 142; function-alist approach, 65; human resource activities, 29–33, 137; participative, 59, 127; power, 48, 58; reforms in technology of, 122–24; relations with labor, 38, 93, 96, 101–3, 119; scientific management applied to, 121–22; training programs for, 123–24; transactions, 93–94. *See also* Business firm(s); Labor-management committees

Mangum, Stephen L., 90–91, 98, 147n.1

Manpower Development and Training Act (U.S., 1926), 96

Margerison, C. J., 3–4

Market, the, 1, 11, 13–18, 29, 43, 114; in centrally planned economy, 55–56; control centered in, 14, 20–21, 34–35, 116, 139, 140, 142; human resource activities, 13–14, 20–28, 30–31, 133–

35, 137–38; institutionalists on, 42, 93–94, 100, 103, 142; market economy, 9–10, 56–57, 74–75, 83–84, 143, 144; and need for trade unions, 110–11; during shift to industrial production, 126. *See also* Free market

Marshall, Ray, 92

Marx and Marxism, 37–41, 45–49, 89, 98–100, 109–10, 114; on alienation, 9, 42, 54–55; compared with classical economics, 56–59; compared with Wisconsin School, 41–42; on conflict, 9–10, 71; on control, 18, 20, 35, 133, 134; on employment relations, 3, 5, 11, 50–55; historical perspective on political science, 78; on human resource utilization, 137; influence on sociology and systems theory, 73–75; North American reaction to, 41–42, 43, 45, 147n.1; reaction to political economists, 51–52; seen as a systems theory, 62–63, 66

Maslowe, A. H., 116

Mayo, Elton, 48, 119–21, 136

Mercantilism, *Wealth of Nations* as attack on, 90–91

Methodology, 10–12, 40–41

Meyer, David, 65

Minimum wage, 33

Minorities, 18, 22, 25, 94

Mobility, labor, 9, 25, 96, 97–98

Monopoly, of unions for Williamson, 105

Monopoly capitalism, 13–14, 19, 35, 55, 56, 58–59

Motivation, 2, 25, 48, 114

Multinational firms, 72–73

Munsterberg, Hugo, 148n.1

Myers, Charles, 4, 92, 98, 101

NAFTA (North American Free Trade Agreement), 80, 95–96, 98

Nationalization of natural resource firms, in third world, 143

National Labor Relations Act (NLRA), 79, 142

Natural resource industries, in third world, 142–43

Negotiation, 11–12, 59, 69, 77, 89, 102, 141; agents' role, 14, 114; breakdown under corporatism, 82; on education vouchers, 22; on human resource activities, 23–25, 28, 30, 32, 34, 133–39; industrial relations as study of, 13–15, 131–32; institutionalist emphasis on, 43–45, 44, 93, 107; relationship to center and structure of control, 13–14, 15–18, 20, 27, 130; role in establishment of public social insurance, 32, 34; role in third-world economic development, 143–45

Neoclassical economics, 13, 25, 39, 73, 90–92, 134; relationship to institutionalism and neo-institutionalism, 2, 44, 61, 103, 104, 112

Neoclassical labor economics, 49, 116, 130

Neo-institutionalism, 5, 92, 103–9, 111–13

Neo-Marxism, 57, 67, 76

Neo-Weberianism, 63–64

New Deal legislation, 79–80

New Harmony community, in Indiana, 66

New International Economic Order (NIEO), 143–44, 148n.4

New Lanark community, in Britain, 66

Nonrevolutionary socialism, 45–46, 110–11

North American Free Trade Agreement (NAFTA), 80, 95–96, 98

Opportunism, Williamson on, 104, 147n.4

Oppression, as factor in interpersonal relationships, 127–28

Organizations, 5, 65–66, 77, 104, 115, 131; as actors in social system, 73; viewed as governments, 82–83. *See also individual organizations*

Overdetermination, in Marxism, 52

Oversupply of labor, 8–9

Owen, Robert, 66

Parkin, Frank, 63–64
Parsons, Talcott, 62, 63, 67–68, 73, 76, 99
Participative management, 59, 127
Paternalism, in Mayo's approach, 120
Pension plans, 32–33, 34, 138
Performance, 25, 73–74
Perlman, Selig, 4, 91, 116
Peron, Juan, 17, 81
Personnel administration, 1, 47, 115, 120, 123–24
Phenomenology, 69
Piece-rate systems, 48, 75
Planned economies. *See* Central planning
Pluralism (European institutionalism), 37–38, 41, 46, 48–49, 67, 80–81; dissent from traditional economics, 91–92; systems theory perspective, 69, 70–71. *See also* Institutional economics
Polanyi, Karl, 7–8, 35, 114, 126
Political science, 25, 56, 61–62, 76–89, 132–33, 137; as element in industrial relations field, 4–5, 10–11, 32, 49, 61, 79–88; on governance structure, 86, 106–8, 109, 113; Marxist reaction to, 51–52
Population growth, third-world, 144–45
Poverty, 7–8, 23
Power, 14, 35, 45, 58–59, 103, 137; of agents, 139; balance of, 9, 38, 94, 127–28; for bargaining, 71, 74–75; of capitalist class for Marx, 37, 53–54; pluralist focus on, 38, 67; role in alienation, 125; as source of conflict, 70–71, 72
Pragmatism, 11, 45, 147n.1
Preindustrial society, 5, 7–8, 68, 83–84, 147n.1
Prices, 51, 74–75; determination, 16, 93; market, 104; theory of, 2, 10
Prince, The (Machiavelli), 78
Principles of Scientific Management (Taylor), 46–47
Private Employment Councils, 23, 147n.4

Production, 66–67, 75–76, 111; changes in technology of, 100, 126–28; control of, 75, 83, 84–85; rationalization of, 121–22; relations of, 42, 50–53, 76
Productivity, 30, 74, 103, 118, 130; Hawthorne effect results, 119–21
Proletariat. *See* Labor; Workers
Promotion process, 22–24, 27, 28, 93
Property, private: employers' rights based on, 85, 86, 87; relationship to income distribution, 143
Protective institutions, 8, 14–15, 43, 75, 90, 128; construction of, 96; control centered in, 19; disillusionment regarding, 129–30; governance structure, 105; in market economy, 8, 17–18; need for in third-world economies, 146; unions as, 107, 110–11. *See also individual institutions*
Psychology, 1–2, 25, 61, 69, 132, 136–37; alienation as a concern of, 125; application to the workplace, 118–22, 126–30; as element in industrial relations field, 4–5, 10, 11, 49, 61, 114–18, 148nn.2, 3

Quality circles, 30, 87, 103, 127, 136
Quality of work life committees, 103, 109
Quotas, hiring, 25–27

Race discrimination, in apprenticeship programs, 24
Rate busting, in piece-rate systems, 75
Rationalization: of personnel function, 123–24; of technical preconditions of work, 121–24, 128
Rationing transaction, 94
Reality: Granovetter and Tilly's theory, 74–75; society as level of, 62, 64–65
Reasonable value, 43, 44–45, 93–95, 104
Repetitive work, effect on autonomy, 125, 127
Resnick, Stephen A., 52

Resources: bargaining rights and power dependent on, 74–75, 84, 147n.1; distribution of as source of conflict, 70; natural, 142–43

Retirement, 44, 138; pension plans, 32–33, 34, 138; and social security system, 32, 34, 137

Revolutionary perspective, 9, 19, 46, 66; Marxist, 38, 40, 42, 51, 55, 133

Rewards, 48, 73–74, 125

Ricardo, David, 90

Rights: and authority relationships, 83–88; of employers, 46, 84–88; of stockholders, 86, 107–9; of workers, 82–84, 147n.1

Roles: for Dahrendorf, 71; work roles, 50–56, 58–59, 115

Roosevelt, Franklin D., 32

Ross, Arthur, 41, 98

Rostow, Walter, 143

Roy, Donald, 75–76

Rules. See Work rules

Safety regulations, 32, 95, 123

Scientific management (Taylorism), 47–48, 121–23, 124, 148n.3

Security, 18, 96, 103, 107, 116–17. See also Insecurity

Shaw, George Bernard, 45, 110

Skills, job. See Jobs; Training

Skinner, B. F., 120, 122

Slavery, 27, 83, 135

Smelser, Neil J., 64–65

Smith, Adam, 7, 13, 16, 57, 58, 90–91

Social behaviorism, 69

Social democracy, 45, 96, 111

Social insurance, 4, 8, 32–33, 45, 147n.1. See also Social security; Unemployment; Worker's compensation

Socialism, 38, 45–46, 55, 79, 96, 110–11; utopian, 66, 67

Social sciences (field and theory), 8, 11, 22, 69–70; on human resource activities, 20–34, 136–37; links with industrial relations theory, 1–6, 34–

38, 48–49, 61, 132, 146. See also Economics; Political science; Psychology; Sociology

Social security, 32; United States, 16, 43, 137–38, 147n.1; 1935 act (U.S.), 32, 34, 79, 97. See also Social insurance

Social system(s), 40–41, 67–68, 71–72, 77, 89. See also Society; Systems theory

Society, 12, 62–65, 67, 70, 78, 115; control mechanisms, 127; corporatist, 82; industrial, 5, 7–8, 41, 139, 141–42; relationships in for Marx, 50–51. See also Class(es); Social system(s)

Sociology, 2, 27, 61–78, 88–89, 122, 132; alienation as concern of, 125; conflict theories, 25; as element in industrial relations field, 1, 4–5, 10, 11, 49, 61; employment relations concerns, 75–77; functionalism, 62–68; on human resource activities, 32, 133–34, 136–37; psychological factors given weight in, 115, 130; systems theory, 61–75

Somers, Gerald, 92

Stability (Equilibrium), 62, 70–71, 100–101, 132

Stages of Economic Growth, The (Rostow), 143

State, the, 77–78; corporatist, 80–82

Steam power, shift to electric power, effects on workers, 126–27

Stockholders, rights, 86, 107–9

Strike(s), 28, 74, 84, 147n.1

Struggle, in employment relations, sociological emphasis on, 70–73

Subsidies, government, 22, 81

Subsistence level: farming, 143; of human resources for Marx, 39, 52–54, 57

Supply and demand, 10, 26, 39, 41, 43–44, 63, 75

Surplus value, 39, 42, 52–53, 56, 58

Sweden, 23, 96, 97, 141

Systems theory, 61–68, 78–79, 114; debate over, 61–62, 68–75

Taylor, Frederick W., 46–48, 121–22, 124, 126
Technology, 117, 125
    changes in, 25, 29–31, 100, 102, 126–30; and convergence hypothesis, 141–42; effects for Marxism, 57–58, 133
    and third-world economic development, 143, 144–45
Tension, 64; biological explanation for, 69–70
Textile industry, union role in strategic decisions, 102
Third world (Developing/less-developed countries), 5, 9, 139, 142–46
Thurow, Lester, 94
Tilly, Charles, 73–75, 76, 136–37
Time and motion studies, 122, 123
Top-down methodology, 10
Trade, international, 39, 81–82, 95–96, 143–44, 148n.4
Trade unionism, 1, 45–46, 110–11. See also Labor unions
Training, employment/job, 12, 20–24, 43, 47, 57–58, 123, 133–34; government role, 12, 16, 21–22, 96–98. See also Development of human resources
Transactions, 43, 91–94, 105–8
Tripartite negotiations, 23, 28, 96, 97
Trust fund, social security, 34
Turner, J. H., 70

Uncertainty, 8, 22, 139, 141
Unemployment, 4, 27, 43–44, 96, 133, 135; compensation, 12, 14, 33–34, 84; insurance, 8, 16, 32–33, 43–44, 96, 137–38
Unions, 1, 45–46, 96, 110–11, 145, 146. See also Labor unions
Union shops, 27, 135
Utilization of human resources/labor, 12, 24, 28–31, 48, 124, 148n.1; for classical economics, 56–57; Marxist emphasis on, 37, 53–56; negotiation

issues, 59, 135–37, 142; in third-world economies, 144–45; for Wisconsin School, 37, 94
Utopian socialism, 66, 67

Value(s), 19, 20–21, 77, 85, 125; conflicts in, 89, 108, 133; of labor, 39–40; reasonable, 43, 44–45, 93–95, 104; surplus, 39, 42, 52–53, 56, 58
Vouchers, educational, 22

Wage rates/wages, 24, 63, 82–83, 102, 104–6, 126
    determination, 25, 56–57, 87, 90, 136–37; negotiation, 18, 25, 43; point system, 93–94
    job ranking according to, 73–74
    Marxist theories on, 39, 52–54, 57
    minimum wage, 33
    scientific management on role in workers' motivation, 47–48
Waldo, Dwight, 77, 78, 79, 82–83
War on Poverty, 23, 97
Wazeter, David L., 65–66
Wealth of Nations, The (Smith), 7, 90–91
Webb, Beatrice, 45, 92, 110–11, 113
Webb, Sidney, 45, 92, 110–11, 113
Weber, Max, 3, 63–64, 66, 67, 73
Welfare state, modern, 1, 96
Wells, H. G., 45
Wever, Kirsten, 65
Wheeler, Hoyt, 69–70, 128
Whyte, William Foote, 119–21, 136
Williamson, Oliver, 92, 103–9
Wilson, E. O., 69–70, 81
Wisconsin School institutionalism, 37, 41–43, 46, 49, 96; analysis of labor-management committees, 101, 103; Commons as initiator, 93–94; compared to institutional labor economists, 99; dissent from traditional economics, 91, 92. See also Institutional economics
Wolff, Richard D., 52
Work, 47, 115; technical preconditions

of, 121–24. *See also* Jobs
Workers, 17–18, 121–24; as actors in
   social system, 62–63, 73–75;
   Marxism on, 9, 52, 62–63; replacement workers, 72; rights, 82–84,
   147n.1. *See also* Labor
Worker's compensation, 14, 16, 32–33,
   43, 137–39
Working conditions, 8, 81, 83, 90, 102,
   136; bargaining over, 25, 87; in
   Owen's utopian communities, 66;

safety, 32, 95, 123
Work role(s), 50–56, 58–59, 115
Work rules, 29–30, 50, 54, 59, 135–36
Works councils, 14, 87, 91–92, 109, 111,
   141; place in human resource
   utilization, 29–31, 136
World economy. *See* International
   economy
Wrong, Dennis, 69

Zone of acceptance of contract, 106–7